WHAT WOMEN WANT

WHAT WOMEN WANT

Evidence from British Social Attitudes

Second Edition

Geoff Dench

With a new introduction by the author

Transaction Publishers
New Brunswick (U.S.A.) and London (U.K.)

First Transaction printing
New material this edition copyright © 2011 by Transaction Publishers, New Brunswick, New Jersey. Originally published in 2010 by the Hera Trust.

This book is printed on acid-free paper that meets the American National Standard for Permanence of Paper for Printed Library Materials.

Library of Congress Catalog Number: 2011012401
ISBN: 978-1-4128-4298-3
Printed in the United States of America

Library of Congress Cataloging-in-Publication Data

Dench, Geoff.
 What women want : evidence from British social attitudes / Geoff Dench.
  p. cm.
 Originally published: London : Hera Trust, 2010.
 ISBN 978-1-4128-4298-3
  1. Women--Great Britain--Social conditions. 2. Women--Employment--Great Britain. 3. Sex role--Great Britain. 4. Women--Family relationships--Great Britain. 5. Single mothers--Great Britain--Social conditions. I. Title.

HQ1593.D46 2011
305.40941'09045--dc22

To Belinda
For her good ideas and endless patience

CONTENTS

Acknowledgements

The *Hera Trust* is grateful to the *Robert Gavron Charitable Trust* for its support of this programme of work, to the *National Centre for Social Research* for copies of BSA survey data and help constructing some of the derived variables used in this analysis, to *Grandparents Plus* for ongoing research collaboration and to the *Centre for Policy Studies* for hosting the series of seminars leading to this report.

Introduction

This report is compiled from four background papers prepared for family policy seminars held at the Centre for Policy Studies, in association with the Hera Trust, during February and early March 2010.

My original idea was to carry out the seminars, note the discussions, do some supplementary reading and then quickly edit the papers into a more coherent document for dissemination during the summer 2010. But that plan was dropped after I realised that what was really interesting was not so much my presentation of or commentary on the data as the data itself. I had no intention of developing the data further, as that could take me very a long time. So I decided that there was no good argument against simply publishing the papers immediately and as they stood.

The chapters of this report are therefore the texts of the papers more or less exactly in the form in which they were prepared for the seminars. The only real change, which is in this second edition but not the first, is the addition of a final table in chapter 4 – table 4.18 – bringing in some later data.

It is not impossible that a further book will materialise eventually, as an outcome of the process originally intended. But if it does, it will not now need to reproduce all of the materials contained in these papers, nor indeed all the arguments. And I will be able to do it at my leisure. It will be a later and substantially different book.

Geoff Dench

London,
April 2010

Introduction to the Transaction Edition

Sociologists need to listen to *all* women

The research report which follows aims to help fill a glaring gap in our understanding of modern Britain. This is necessary because the last couple of decades have not been British Sociology's finest hour. A popular new sexual division of labour has been established here—as it has in many other countries. However, instead of analysing its characteristics impartially and examining how it fits in with other aspects of national life, many British sociologists have sneered at it and seem to be doing their best to impede it. Their behaviour has been a bad performance, one that does not serve the best interests of sociology.

I believe that a sexual division of labour is valuable. As I have argued elsewhere, it is probably what makes human society distinctive.[1] We all used to understand this. Traditional ideas about the sexual composition of society appreciate that women are the central sex, because family life and reproduction are the fundamental processes around which society revolves. For their part, men are seen as rather marginal and problematic. As among other advanced 'social' species, adult males left to their own devices tend to hover near the edge of communities—ready to help with insemination but not much else. They are potentially quite a nuisance. What has been important in human cultural development is the extent to which useful things have been found for men to do, to bring most of them into full and constructive group membership.

Generally, this has been achieved by giving men specific responsibilities in families in return for regularised sexual access and other rewards. Their duties have concentrated around those tasks which women themselves have been least keen or able to carry out. Both sexes benefit from this division of labour. Men themselves are brought into more orderly and civilised existences; and in the process they become (half) useful to women and can help to prevent them from becoming overburdened. All of this requires the collective disciplining of men, however. Almost invariably, it involves making their full membership in the community *conditional* on the successful performance of obligations on behalf of a family. In most societies, this also entails some distinction between those essential activities which are carried out within the family home and performed mainly by women, and those which are done in the public realm, mainly by men.

Until relatively recently, this mechanism for transforming men into useful family members and citizens appears to have worked reasonably well, promoting sexual interdependence and harmony. However, this seems to have been based on a presumption that the private realm of family and community life—the domain of women—was the real heart of society, and that men's activities could be seen as *serving* this realm. Consequently, as society and the state have become increasingly complex, and public realm roles have increased in status and grown more powerful, it has become harder for women to remain satisfied with their lot. Discontent has grown. At the same time, progressive refinements in birth control technologies have freed women to spend more of their own time in the public realm if they so choose. Thus, over the last century or so, some modernisation and re-balancing of the sexual division of labour has become necessary.

Unfortunately, the way that this modernisation and re-balancing has happened, in Britain at any rate, seems to have occurred at the expense of sexual interdependence and overall social harmony. Advocates of sexual symmetry, who deny any sexual differences in basic orientations, have had the upper hand, and have concentrated public policy on maximising women's participation in the public realm by arguing for their *individual* rights. They have treated the predominance of men in this realm as evidence of gender discrimination, and see this as operating with the support of patriarchal family relationships that prevent women from being able to function effectively. Progress out of this is to be achieved through the use of state power, in order to eliminate any direct male privileges and to also ensure that the private realm of family work—now often characterised publicly as no more than chores—is shared equally between men and women. In its rejection of any sexual division of labour this emerging libertarian strategy is turning out to be a *conflict* model of society. It casts men and women as opposed groups of individuals, with similar basic drives and interests, who are competing for dominance. There is little room in it for ideas about sexual interdependence.

This mission fits the aspirations of those middle class women who have important careers open to them, offering economic independence; but not of working class women who don't. There have been considerable class differences in the need for a change in values. Women from poor backgrounds have long been used to taking paid jobs when they are able, to supplement family incomes. For these women, the traditional emphasis placed on men as *sole* family providers has always been largely irrelevant. A change of values was actually more pertinent to better-off families, among whom the idea of women taking paid work had previously been resisted as denoting poverty and lack of choice. It is in this milieu that improved control of reproduction has raised the possibility of a *career*, and hence greater personal independence.

In spite of these rather different class implications, most British sociologists were quick to embrace the new, libertarian model as a vision of social progress and justice for *all* sectors of society. This stance was almost certainly linked with their own collective incorporation into the postwar meritocratic elite in Britain, and the adoption of a professional role within it of looking after vulnerable citizens. This corporate social mobility seems to have affected sociologists' ability to take a critical and independent view. There has been a significant abandonment by them of interest in ordinary family and community life, which were once dominant concerns. Those themes have been replaced by an overwhelming fascination with personal freedom and the welfare state, and the needs of categories of citizens conceptualised as groups of free individuals with shared interests. The most important *relationships* recognised in this conceptual framework are those between citizens and the state itself.

This perspective needs to change. While sociology has been looking the other way, ordinary families have carried on trying to cope as interdependent *groupings*, in an institutional environment that has proved to be increasingly hostile. They can see that the consequences of competition between men and women in the job market have been harmful to family and community life; and moreover that this has been most evident in regards to the working class.

The available evidence indicates that for men with satisfying, well-paid jobs, the entry of more women into the workforce has simply raised the stakes. Middle-class men are working even longer hours, and even harder, and avoiding marriage and family responsibilities even more resolutely than before in order to succeed. So middle-class mothers with careers of their own are heavily over-burdened. Thus for this social strata, feminist strategy has gone some way to actually create the enemy it defined at the outset—the selfish, workaholic man who both tries to exclude women from the job market and fails to pull his weight in the private realm. This outcome has not helped women, though it has arguably been good for the cause, in that the disappointments of these career women appear to be fuelling feminist strategy. Most such women do stay with their partners, as the meagre support this situation provides does make a difference. But they suffer, and grumble.

Elsewhere in society, replacement of interdependence with competition has been comprehensively bad for families. It liberates men, not women; and may thereby be causing centuries of civilisation to unravel. Among those men whose only possible jobs are menial—and hardly worth taking on unless dignified by a family cause—a common response to the official line that women want more opportunities to work themselves seems to be to stand back and let them get on with it. Hence the twin surges in male unemployment and single motherhood. Growing numbers of working class mothers who want male providers can't find unattached men who are employed. And many potential male providers have little incentive to take available jobs, as they have no family role. This is what happens to men when we treat work as something an individual may choose to do, rather than something which needs to be done for the sake of groups. Men's contribution to families and communities has plummeted, while their general failure to play a positive role in society continues to grow.

Without family responsibilities to humanise and domesticate them, more men are slipping into disorganised behaviour. They know that they are more dispensable than women. So when they no longer feel needed many just drift back to the margins of society. This is not a problem *for men* themselves—who are less of a social entity than often imagined. It does, however, mean that men have become more of a problem *for society*. This situation is blighting the lives of communities where a few generations earlier these men would have been valued and made useful. The ballooning prison population, the increasing number of unskilled unemployed and under-motivated schoolboys, the escalating rate of male suicide—all signify a serious breakdown of the social order, more or less as predicted by Charles Murray.[2]

The ordinary women who have witnessed this collapse of community life have not been drawn by this experience to feminism and celebration of government policy. On the contrary, they have become more explicit in their enthusiasm for traditional values and sexual divisions. Outside the middle and upper classes, most women in Britain have grown up in communities where women have always had to have paid work, certainly before having children, in order to supplement family income. Following the replacement in polite society of the convention that women should not work, by feminist injunctions that they *should* work, ordinary women have simply updated their own traditions and adopted them as a new formal expectation. Thus at the popular level we now have a revised sexual division of labour whereby most women do anticipate working, though not fulltime once they have children as they still prefer to give priority to family life. However, they no longer feel supported by this by state policies.

There is a place for men as main providers in the new division of labour, and so it retains valuable sexual interdependence. Many women have discovered for themselves that men need *women* and families, to furnish their motivations in the private realm, every bit as much as women may need *men* economically. For them feminist mantras about the importance of avoiding dependence on a man no longer have much resonance. But these policy refrains do seem to have a discouraging effect on *men*. Thus the new model of interdependence remains in some tension with state policy, and as a result may be less effective than it could be. The official goal of dismantling all obstacles to women's success in the labour market seems to be directly at odds with strategies needed to protect ordinary family life.

The report which follows attempts to explore these issues in more detail than is usual, by examining women's responses collected over the last twenty-five years in the UK's leading annual survey, *British Social Attitudes*. This survey contains a valuable combination of behavioural and attitudinal questions. The resulting data show clearly that although women in Britain have continued to increase their overall participation in the job market, this does not mean that they have become less concerned about their families. For a while it did appear as if women might be transferring their main attention to the world of work. During the 1980s the growing number of middle-class women entering the labour market showed a declining interest in family life. New Labour decided to ride this trend, in a bid to capture the middle ground of British politics. So at the end of the 1980s, and through the early 1990s, it carried out a sustained campaign to appeal to working women; and for a while this did lead to—or at least coincide with—a general rise in belief that work was the principal means whereby all citizens, male and female, could make their contribution to society.

However, this attitude soon peaked, and then went into decline. Approximately a year after Labour gained power (in 1997), and started to push policies to promote women's paid work, women themselves began to react against the experience of full-time working. Although the proportions of women in work have stayed buoyant since then, there has been a decline in their support for the idea that this is a good thing and a revival of the enthusiasm—especially among younger cohorts who lead changes of attitudes in these areas—for more traditional lives and values. Many have been struck by the deterioration in family and community life in Britain in recent years, and in the wellbeing of children, and are coming to see women's traditional role in the private realm as being more important to society than paid jobs. Those women who are happiest now are those only working part-time—that is, with one foot in the world of work but also with plenty of time to spend with their children and in other 'private realm' activities.

Having a working partner (as main provider) is an important factor underpinning this new lifestyle; and what is also clear from the figures is that single mothers—who in the British context are mainly very dependent on the state, which gives them financial support on the understanding that they will work as soon as they can—are the *least* happy category of women. So it is not surprising that there is declining support among ordinary women for policies designed to promote gender equality in the workplace. As Catherine Hakim has often pointed out—usually to be howled down by other sociologists—it is more important for most women that their partners and sons pursue reasonably unimpeded careers than for them to enjoy full economic parity with men themselves.[3] Full parity in the workplace is something that is only really sought by middle class women who are strongly attached to their careers.

The problem is that these are the only women who seem to be able to get the ear of influential sociologists in Britain. We now have a position where the policy advice given by sociologists seems to be based simply on the perspectives and interests of a powerful minority of women—including leading sociologists themselves. This is unfortunate for both ordinary families and sociology—particularly for sociology, as it is undermining its voice and role in this area, and by extension other areas too. For their part, ordinary families will probably get what they need in the end. Policymakers cannot continually ignore popular feelings in a democracy; they will simply find themselves out of power.

Indeed, there is some intriguing evidence emerging of the declining electoral appeal of feminism, which should strike fear into the hearts of (or impose some reason upon) even the most resolute of feminist warriors. It is now becoming apparent just how badly New Labour's denial of the popularity of sexual divisions, and its related hostility to traditional family life, may have eroded morale in its political heartlands. As this report details, if we look at those women who are the backbone of local community life then we notice a very serious collapse in their support for the Labour Party since the party started to court working women.

Strategists in the main parties may well feel that this is not very important, on the grounds that housewives and stay-at-home mothers are a dying breed. That would be a mistake. All the available evidence points to an ongoing revival of enthusiasm among younger women for these roles, and of a renewed recognition by them of their social importance. It is hard to avoid the conclusion that Labour's dedication to the interests of working women has alienated a section of the electorate just as it is starting to become significant once more. This will surely influence election manifestoes eventually; and then obstacles to ordinary family life will start to disappear.

However, it is not so clear that British Sociology can recover. It seems to have traded its critical capacities in order to secure a cosy role within Britain's (self-proclaimed) modernising elite. The danger now is that if it becomes widely seen as having lost its ability to understand what is actually happening in the world, it will not be considered much use to *anyone*. I suggest it needs to study the findings in the report below with a sense of urgency!

Geoff Dench
London
February 2011

Notes

[1]   *Transforming Men*; Transaction 1996
[2]   *Losing Ground*, 1984
[3]   Most recently in *Feminist Myths and Magic Medicine*

WHAT WOMEN WANT: SUMMARY

1   A woman's work
It is commonly assumed that women in Britain have given up their domestic lives, in order to take fuller part in the labour market, without any regrets. But this does not seem to be the case. There has indeed been greater agreement by women in recent years with values asserting that women should be free to work if they want to, and that they *can* do it. And these are the sort of findings that usually get publicised. However, over the last five to ten years (depending on the exact issue) there has also been increasing approval by women for propositions stating that women really want a home and children more than a job, that family life suffers if women work and that being a housewife is a rewarding role.

So there are clear signs of a revival of enthusiasm for traditional women's concerns. This is most evident among mothers, and in particular *young* mothers. However, it does coincide with currently very high employment rates for young mothers, so that it need not be taken as meaning that mothers do not want to work at all. It is more realistic to see it as simply confirming that work does not mean the same thing for women as for men. For most women, paid work is still something that is taken on for the benefit of their families, and to be fitted around their needs. That is why part-time working is so popular. The happiest women are those who have part-time jobs with plenty of time to be housewives and mothers too. There is no great appetite for competing with men in the job market; indeed women's rediscovered interest in home life and community shows that most of them do want men to be the *main* breadwinners.

What many women seem to be remembering is that the most important social processes are those taking place in the private realm of families and communities. Men are less effective in that domain. So that is where women's distinctive contribution needs to be.

2 The value of a male partner

The proportion of mothers living without a male partner continues to rise in Britain. This process has commonly been understood to mean that women want to be independent of men. This may once have been the case, but it does not fit the emerging pattern. At a time when most women are not becoming mothers until older (than they used to be), and more are carrying on paid work after doing so, *single* mothers are becoming younger and doing *less* paid work. And whereas in the past single mothers typically would have been married, or cohabited for some time before being alone, an increasing proportion now have never lived with a partner, and have instead just gone straight into being lone mothers. Divergence of lifestyles is taking place.

What the data suggest is that women who want to work and have careers have realised that they stand the best chance of doing so if they have a husband. Those women who are now becoming lone mothers appear to be those who don't really want to work, but to *have children*. They have very traditional female desires, and values: but they cannot find a marriageable man. They know however that in Britain the welfare state will itself take on the role of provider, for the sake of the children.

Government policy in Britain is still based on the assumptions of twenty years ago. It makes no sense now to treat single mothers as women who need help until they find paid work. The pressure on them to find work is just making many of them miserable. It would be better to acknowledge that most single mothers want mainly to be mothers and housewives, and to put resources into helping more *men* into work so that they become useful and acceptable as husbands.

3 Wider family ties – and grandparents

In Britain as other countries it is extended family networks which provide the main framework for reciprocal personal supports between people. As these families have become slimmer (with more generations, but fewer people in each generation) the part played by grandparents has become more salient.

The greater involvement of women in the labour market is however changing the way that these families operate. Women who have invested in a career are reluctant to give up paid work, in favour of childcare, when they become grandmothers. They relied on their own mothers becoming babushkas for them when they were young mothers themselves. But now it makes more sense for many of them to stay on at work and give money in lieu of childcare services. This also fits in with the greater interest many young mothers now have in looking after their own children. So families are showing themselves able to adjust to changing work patterns.

What they may find harder to accommodate is the extension of single motherhood into the grandmother generation. There are now a growing number of extended families without men. A lone mother with conventional married parents can stay in touch with mainstream society, where she can hope to find both a partner and, when she is ready, a job. But extended families without men seem much more inward-looking. Such families may be good at giving care to children. But often they do not do much else, and are materially dependent on working families (via the welfare system) for their survival. They are the first clear sign of an underclass developing in Britain.

4 Representing women

Now that women are more involved in the marketplace and politics, they expect to speak directly for themselves rather than through men. But paradoxically this may mean that ordinary women, especially ordinary mothers, have effectively lost their voice. The values of those women who are in a position to have any influence are not the same as most women's (and indeed are often more like men's).

This matters because the main political parties are losing touch with what most women actually think. Only middle-class career women can be sure of getting an ear. There are many ordinary women, including single mothers, who feel alienated from contemporary Britain because of its abandonment of traditional family values and neglect of communities. They are increasingly turning their back on the mainstream political parties; and this is helping to boost extremist parties like the BNP who do still respect these values.

It is time for policymakers to start listening to ordinary women. They are the ones who know what is really going on in Britain.

And it is the Labour Party which most needs to listen to them, as it appears to be that party which has been losing support from ordinary women most heavily as a result of its neglect of families and local community life.

CHAPTER 1   A WOMAN'S WORK

Destiny through paid work

It is one of the ruling clichés of modern Britain that women's lives –
and those of their families – have been transformed by their
increased participation in the labour market; and triumphalist
commentaries like in the *Economist* a few weeks ago tell us that the
process will be continuing for quite a while.[1] But what does this all
mean? Is it what women themselves actually want? And insofar as it
has already happened, why has it done so, and what are the
implications? Underlying this bland cliché there is a boiling cauldron
of unresolved issues and differing opinions about what is desirable.
It is perhaps the danger of becoming engulfed in these which makes
use of the safe cliché so popular. However, I feel that it is high time
that we explored and aired some of the questions that are bubbling
away below the surface. Our collective failure to do so is one of the
main factors feeding the political alienation which is currently
poisoning British public life.

For there are serious misunderstandings circulating at the moment,
about women and work, which need to be cleared up. Harriet
Harman's *Women and Work Commission* continues to ratchet up the
pressure to remove all possible obstacles to full equality for women
in the labour market. But much of what is assumed by policymakers
is already very out of date, and fails to address important concerns.
This is why I want to explore these issues. It is also one of the
reasons why I am using *British Social Attitudes* data to do so. In our
rather technocratic era, BSA findings are what come closest to an
accepted voice of ordinary Britons.[2] You and I may know something
very well; but until it has been picked over and clarified and
disseminated by *British Social Attitudes* then our political leaders are
able to claim that nobody has *told them*. These issues *have* been
examined by BSA; but rather less has been done to publicise the
findings than is desirable. That is why I feel the need to act.

Careers for women

I want to start by sketching out, very briefly, what I feel are some key issues here. First of all it perhaps needs to be spelt out that when we refer to increased participation of women in the labour market what we are actually talking about is the development of *careers* for women. It is misleading to assume that women in the past did not have any job market experience. Most did, of course. It was one of the felt privileges of being a middle class woman that one did *not* need to. It was the others who worked. So when I hear people saying that 'women' in Britain now work, it reminds me of the opening passage in Toby Young's 'How to lose friends and alienate people', where his boss, the editor of a society magazine, on hearing that a plane has just crashed, asks "Anyone on board?"

For what is meant by 'working' in this context is that women now have a chance to do more interesting work, and pursue proper careers alongside men. Therefore high status women can join in. And this is indeed a recent development, which could not have happened until certain *other* developments (for example in the reliable regulation of reproduction) had themselves taken place.

But just as important here as the pill has I think been the cultural evolution of the idea that we are all made by our work. Following the Second World War, British governments found that they needed to adopt new models of social cohesion to replace the broken structures which were crumbling with the empire. A popular notion was that in a properly open society every citizen should have the chance to contribute to the common wellbeing through doing what they were best at, and then be individually rewarded by society for that. 'Everyone' most definitely included women, who were regarded by progressive thinkers such as Eleanor Rathbone as having been too long confined to domesticity, on the margins of society, by male domination of the centre.[3] So in the years following the 1948 Education Act, girls with lively minds were encouraged to turn their backs on the private realm of family and local community life, and to aspire to a real job alongside male fellow-citizens.

These processes played a significant role in nurturing the libertarian

2

values which exploded onto the scene in the 1960s, and have driven subsequent changes in British society. The 1960s were the period when young women started to enter higher education in large numbers, when their expectations of work began routinely to encompass serious careers, and when employers had to start adjusting.[4] The vanguard generation which pioneered this change have since been dubbed the baby boomers. They will be discussed at various points in the coming argument; but what stands out as particularly important about them is their boundless faith in the capacity of the public realm, that is political and economic institutions, to be moved by values that women respect and to provide suitably moral solutions for social problems. With the rise of the baby boomers, the public realm became able to take on the functions of - and so take over - the private. This made it imperative for women to become part of it, and arguably moved the focus of their concerns as women *out* of the private domain. This leads into the second introductory point that I want to make, which I think is far more substantial.

Career versus community

Most accounts of women's increasing attachment to public realm institutions and values fail to draw any attention to what it is that they may be leaving behind. The recent piece in The Economist is not alone in regarding motherhood simply as a problem for them. It is as if women had existed previously in some sort of social void, from which paid work and full individual citizenship had finally rescued them. But, of course, as we all know at another level, this was not the case. The traditional lifestyle of middle class women (those who have been most affected by the rise of careers) revolved around family and community life within a private realm which for most people – men and women alike – was the undisputed hub of social life. Within this domain women did much (unpaid) work. But at the same time they had a lot of autonomy, and also exercised a good deal of power, especially as wives and mothers. To abandon this would not be a simple and self-evident gain.

Marriage was a central feature of this lifestyle. This was not only by virtue of creating a wide network of kinship ties, entailing reciprocal supports, but also through sustaining a sexual division of labour in

3

which men and women were interdependent, and which gave both of them a place in the community.[5] But interdependence implies difference; and so marriage was one of the first aspects of traditional British society to be deemed detrimental to women by postwar modernisers. Geoffrey Gorer, writing in 1955, gives an appreciative analysis of the complementary aspects of the husband/wife relationship which was at the hub of conventional British community life.[6] But when he updated his study just a few years later he had to note that complementarity was rapidly being replaced by a new, egalitarian mode in which companionship provided the bond.[7] And by the 1980s, when baby boomers had moved into influential positions throughout British public life, this view had become publicly dominant.

The transition of women's energy and concern into the public realm has generally been represented as a benefit for all – with rights and independence for women, and their civilising influence in business and politics for the rest of us. Few influential voices can be heard lamenting the decline of the private domain, and loss of the autonomy which disappears with it. Instead we have seen the emergence of new conventions which treat even family-based activities of women as being performed *for* society as a whole (in order to qualify them for this or that state benefit). This leads us to some confusing places. Some years ago for example, when grappling with the problem of how to ensure that mothers might continue to enjoy the high status that they had possessed formerly, when they had been at the heart of a vibrant private realm, Arnold Toynbee came up with the highly problematic formula that the state should pay them (at a suitably high rate) for their social contribution:

> *Insofar as, and for as long as, she serves society as a mother, I feel sure that a woman ought to be given the high status and big salary that the key profession of motherhood deserves. Her status ought to be at least as high as, say, a professor's or a magistrate's or a pilot's, and her salary ought to be of a corresponding size.* (Arnold Toynbee, 1989, p. 118)

The idea that women do or should become mothers, and care for kin, in order to serve wider society (and be paid by it) is possibly one of the most muddling social policy notions to have arisen in Britain in modern times. But once the priority of the public realm has been asserted, this sort of thing follows.

Monitoring progress

Meanwhile, most actual public concern about women in recent decades has been about how they are faring within the labour market. Thus, during the 1970s, anxiety that women were encountering unfair obstacles in the job market led to extensive equal employment opportunity legislation. Then an influential study carried out in 1980 highlighted the continuing problems related to working which arose from women's attachment to their roles as wives and mothers.[8] So in the early 1980s attention was given to the domestic arrangements which still seemed to be limiting women's chances of behaving as free citizens. The hunt for New Man, who could help to unlock the door, was on.

All this helped to stimulate the emergence in 1983 of a new national opinion survey – *British Social Attitudes* – devoted to documenting and analysing people's changing lives in modern Britain.[9] The great interest aroused by BSA's early findings relating to women and work enabled the survey to secure the funding to establish itself as an annual event. So during its first decade, it carried many questions about working women and their families, reflecting the debates (and domestic battles) that were taking place nationally at the time.

By the middle of the 1990s, BSA had accumulated a wide range of other interests too, and was contracted to a number of government departments (Health, Transport, Environment etc) to run regular batches of questions for them. So there has been rather less about working women since then. However, by the 2008 survey a full generation of material had been amassed, making it possible to start carrying out a reasonably long-term assessment of change. There is more than enough collected now to permit more extensive and considered analysis of the implications of the idea of the female career – 60 years on from the 1948 Education Act – including some treatment of the central question of how far this is (still) what women want. *British Social Attitudes* is the perfect place to explore this question, as it has been so closely involved with the subject for so many years, and contains such a variety of other materials against which it can be analysed.

Analysing BSA data

In truth there is far too much data assembled now for any quick or easy analysis to be made. So what I have done here inevitably constitutes only a first skim, to get a taste of what is there. Because of this, I have given priority to documenting basic questions about 'who thinks or does what'. Fancier interpretations of why, and in what circumstances, have been postponed. And there are still limits to what can be done anyway.

Firstly, it was not until 2001 that BSA schedules began regularly to contain questions enabling the identification of the respondents who are parents – as I have recently reported.[10] Before then, as in most other major surveys in recent decades, the only parents who were identifiable as such were those co-resident with dependent children at the time of the fieldwork. Relatively little interpretative analysis was possible. In the course of analysing the data since 2001, I discovered that another question (referring to 'responsibility for bringing up children') which is present for most years before 2001 does serve as a very good proxy for a direct parenthood question. That is, when run against direct questions on being a parent, the 'responsibility' question proves pretty reliable in identifying parents of older children no longer sharing the parental home.[11] So for those years before 2001 when there was no direct question on being a parent I have used this indirect identifier instead.

Secondly, very few variables other than those dealing with demographic and socio-economic characteristics recur every year. Most of the detailed examinations of working women's lives were carried out in the early surveys, when public interest in these issues was at its height. But a few questions have subsequently been repeated, at intervals, and these are what make longer-term analysis possible. Since about 1990 several key questions have been re-run on a four-year cycle. So I have structured my own analysis here around that pattern, by using the sequence of key years to provide the basic framework for measuring change in attitudes. During the mid-80s there were many questions asked; and relatively few of them have

6

been repeated much. Some of the latter were run in (or near) 1986, so that is the first of my key years. The other years are 1990, 1994, 1998, 2002 and 2006, when modules of questions on women and work were included in the survey.

To assist interpretation of the attitudinal materials, it is useful to have a corresponding time framework for background data covering the demographic and work characteristics of respondents. I decided not simply to select those same years. This is because there is always a certain amount of sampling variability between surveys, as well as short term change, which creates uneven flows and patterns. Where the data is available for every year, as it is for these basic characteristics, it is worth pooling together several years and producing averages for those periods. I have done this for four-year periods, to fit in as nearly as possible with the 'key years' in which attitudinal materials appear. This gives larger and extremely reliable samples and, especially for the earlier years, smoothes out flows. There were no BSA surveys in 1988 and 1992; so I could not simply take four year blocks. The groupings that I have used are therefore as follows. To back up year '1986' in the key year sequence, I have pooled background data from years 1983 to 1986. For year '1990', I have pooled data from 1987, 1989, 1990 and 1991 (listed in tabulations as 1987-91). From 1993 onwards the pattern is simpler. Key year '1994' is backed by data for years 1993-96; '1998' is backed by 1997-2000; '2002' by 2001-04 and '2006' by 2005-08.

The data used stops at 2008 for background data, and 2006 for key attitude questions. This cut-off is helpful because it means that there is no chance of the current recession being responsible for the findings. (There is a slight possibility of a few late summer interviews in 2008, after the start of the credit crunch, influencing that year's findings very marginally. But as data for that year is pooled into a 4-year block, and averaged, any such influence will be negligible.) This is important, as it means all of the trends identified and discussed here are almost certainly part of longer-term social changes, rather than just reactions to temporary economic conditions. The recession may well intensify (or perhaps even interrupt) some of these trends, but at least I shall not have to try to unscramble all that *here*!

Valuing work

The rising tide

We will begin the analysis of BSA data by looking at how the movement to regard paid work as the heartbeat of modern society fits in with women's social attitudes and values. The first batch of data that I want to introduce here is that relating to the importance attached by women to having paid jobs themselves.

Table 1.1 Women's changing attitudes to family and work. a
Steady or continuing measures

(% of All women)	1986	1990	1994	1998	2002	2006
% agree with pro-domestic values						
A man's job is to earn money; a woman's job is to look after the home and family*	43	23	22	17	15	15
A pre-school child is likely to suffer if his or her mother works		42	34		31	30
% agree with pro-work values						
A working mother can establish just as warm and secure relationship with her children as a mother who does not work		56	70		71	70
Having a job is the best way for a woman to be an independent person*	66	55	60		54	
Base range	*1499*	*1225-1323*	*502-528*	*479*	*1064-1093*	*941-987*

* These questions not asked in 1986. Figures given here are the averages from pooled 1984 and 1987 data.

The main story emerging here is how women indeed have come to value work more than they did; though it should be noted that what many women seem to have responded to most avidly is not so much the idea that they ought to work as that they should be allowed to do so if that is what they freely choose – as opposed to following (outmoded and restrictive) social conventions.

Over the years, BSA (along with other surveys) have used a number of standardised attitude questions to measure women's growing valuation of the public realm and diminishing concern about the social costs of working. This first table here (1.1) collects together some of these measures to give an idea of how they have fared over the last couple of decades. The first measure in it, dealing with prescriptive sex roles, charts a continuing shift away from prescription towards a libertarian position in which women are free to work if they want. In the late 1980s the pace of this change was extremely rapid.[12] This must have involved many women consciously changing their minds. Since the mid 1990s the rate of change has been much slower, and can now be accounted for by cohort replacement – whereby older women attached to traditional ideas are replaced by younger who are not.[13]

Political mobilisation

I need to digress briefly at this point to note that in the mid to late 1980s many in the Labour Party were realising that giving stronger support to working women could help the party fully update itself (as New Labour) and capture a bigger share of the female vote. At the end of the decade, and in the early 1990s, IPPR produced a series of reports written by prominent advocates of working women such as Patricia Hewitt (then Deputy Director at IPPR), Harriett Harman and Anna Coote.[14] These reports coincided with and perhaps helped to orchestrate a notable shift of attitudes among women (and not a few men). This period is, accordingly, when the strongest movement of opinion in favour of women prioritising paid work can be detected. The election success in 1997 of New Labour, and pro-work policies adopted subsequently by that administration, were partly built on this campaign.

9

To return to Table 1.1, the second measure (not fielded until 1990) shows a rapid, early decline in the proportion of women fearing that work would harm children, followed again by a decelerating rate of change. The third backs this up by indicating a corresponding growth in the numbers confident that maternal relationships could be sustained by working mothers; while the fourth (which unfortunately does not come up to the present day) suggests that personal independence has been a continuing consideration for women – though perhaps one which passed its peak some time ago.

This last variable is nevertheless quite significant because, while it puts a very positive gloss on working (as a source of personal independence) it shows how rapidly the early appeal of paid work may have worn off. Once we look at questions which refer directly to the pleasures of private realm activities then the rather limited appeal of paid work quickly becomes evident. Table 1.2 considers some further measures, where support for work itself peaked some years ago and appreciation of the private realm is now reviving.

Table 1.2 Women's changing attitudes to family and work. b
Measures bottoming-out or already reversing

(% of All women)

	1986	1990	1994	1998	2002	2006
% agree with pro-domestic values						
All in all, family life suffers when the woman has a full-time job		43	34	27	34	36
A job is all right, but what most women really want is a home and children*	31	30	23		22	31
Being a housewife is just as fulfilling as working for pay**		45	42		48	50
Watching children grow up is life's greatest joy**		83	79		81	82
Base range	677	715-1319	471-532	473	1091-1101	984-999

* Question not asked in 1986. This figure from 1987 survey.
** Questions not asked in 1990. These figures from 1989 survey.

This second batch of measures all use formulations in which more positive views on traditional female concerns are presented. Responses to the first, which sets full-time work against 'family life' (in the round), suggest that enthusiasm for work reached its summit around the beginning of Tony Blair's administration and has slipped since then – possibly as more women have experienced for themselves the consequences of working full-time. The second, directly counter-posing home and children as an alternative to paid work, shows a similar pattern – with a return in 2006 to levels of approval for domesticity which had not been recorded since 1986.

The third measure, even more provocatively, calls up the traditional notion of a 'housewife'. There are no findings for this variable earlier than 1990. But it is noteworthy that support for domesticity shown through it in 2002 was already greater than that in 1990, and by 2006 had firmed up even further. Perhaps it would have scored highly in 1986 if the question had been put then. The fourth measure, on watching children grow up, shows very little change over the period it covers. It might possibly be seen as additional evidence for a revival of domestic enthusiasm. Certainly it can be read as indicating that even during the high point of pro-work values women have continued to be fascinated by children.

Throughout this period indeed the presence of children in a household has been a major consideration for women when deciding whether paid work is appropriate. Table 1.3 contains responses to a set of questions concerning what women ought to do in certain types of family situation. There has been very little change since 1990 in support for the view that women should work full-time before having children. When she has pre-school children, there is very little support indeed for full-time working, although part-time work is seen as OK (and that endorsement has grown steadily). Basically, though, most women until quite recently have felt that a mother with young children ought to stay at home with them. Once all children are at school, there is more acceptance of working – although still mainly on a part-time basis. And after children have all grown up, there is once again general agreement that full-time working is appropriate. (From 1994, however, agreement on this last point has fallen a bit, perhaps reflecting growing expectations around that time that older women should be available to look after grandchildren. This issue is explored in chapter three.)

Table 1.3 Women's views on when it is appropriate to work

(% of All women)   (Question first asked in 1990)

	1990	1994	1998	2002	2006
Do you think that women should work outside the home full-time, part-time or not at all under these circumstances?					
A. AFTER MARRYING AND BEFORE THERE ARE CHILDREN:					
Work full-time	81	83		81	
Work part-time	10	8		6	
Stay home	2	1		1	
Don't know/n.a.	7	8		12	
B. WHEN THERE IS A CHILD UNDER SCHOOL AGE:					
Work full-time	4	6		4	3
Work part-time	30	32		36	39
Stay home	57	51		46	37
Don't know/n.a.	9	11		14	21
C. AFTER THE YOUNGEST STARTS SCHOOL:					
Work full-time	16	16		15	22
Work part-time	68	66		67	56
Stay home	7	6		4	2
Don't know/n.a.	9	12		14	20

D. AFTER THE CHILDREN LEAVE HOME:				
Work full-time	68	60	60	
Work part-time	19	23	21	
Stay home	2	1	1	
Don't know/n.a.	11	16	18	
Bases	*1322*	*536*	*1108*	*1011*

However, in all sections of this table (especially the last, 'D') there is a manifest rise over time in 'Don't Know' responses. This complicates the interpretation of data. For it may indicate that respondents themselves are increasingly confused or ambivalent – or possibly that they feel out of step with public or official opinion, and may be reluctant to reveal what they actually think.

Choosing paid work

Rising evaluations of paid work by women appear to have gone hand in hand with an increase in their actual labour market participation (though the revival of domestic values since has not been marked by a commensurate *reduction*). The increase in paid employment began during the 1960s, and gathered pace considerably during the 1970s.[15] But it still had a long way to go after 1983. So BSA data are useful in interpreting trends since then. Table 1.4 gives an overview of what they show for the period 1983-2008.

The figures confirm a substantial rise in the numbers of women in paid work; but the process is not even. The 1993-96 period shows no real rise at all (that is, which is large enough to survive the rounding of percentages!), because the 1993 recession had quite an impact on women's jobs. This was then made up under New Labour after 1997. What is even more striking in this table though is the decline of housewives, that is women who define their occupation in private realm terms, as looking after the home. Their numbers fell from 35% of all women in the mid 1980s to 15% twenty years later.

Table 1.4 Women's changing economic status. a All women
(Pooled periods; rounded percentages)

% Women who are:-	1983-86	1987-91	1993-96	1997-00	2001-04	2005-08
Working	41	45	45	49	53	50
Inactive	10	10	12	11	11	11
Retired	14	16	17	20	20	24
Looking after home	35	29	26	20	16	15
Base total	*4486*	*6321*	*7798*	*6326*	*8059*	*9608*

There is also a strong movement over this period to greater longevity, shown here by the growing proportion of *retired* women. An interesting aspect of this is that whereas in 1983 many older women saw themselves as housewives, by 2008 the majority of women over 60 defined themselves in public realm, labour market terms – as retired. The presence of these older women perhaps obscures the main trends in work. So in order to examine these more closely, we need to focus here on working age women. This is done in table 1.5.

Concentration on working age women, plus splitting the work data between full and part-time working, shows up a number of effects more clearly. Firstly, the 1993 recession and its aftermath had a greater impact on full-time than on part-time paid work, producing a small decline for 1993-96 compared with a mere slowing of the rate of increase in part-time work. The growth of part-time working is clearly a success story for the whole period under consideration here. From the mid 1980s to late 1990s it increased about 30%, compared with around 10% for full-time employment. And it has remained steady since. Full-time work has not only gone up relatively less, but has been quite wobbly – with small falls back in 1993-96 and again in the most recent period 2005-08. This last fall is not to do with our new recession, as 2008 figures are no smaller than for 2007. But, given what happened after 1993, it seems very likely that there will be further falls in female employment in the coming years. There is a slow but steady rise in female 'inactivity' across the whole period. This is mainly unemployment, which is a measure of the extent to which women are increasingly reliant on the state for their economic security. More about this in chapter two!

Table 1.5 Women's changing economic status. b Working age women
(Pooled periods; rounded percentages)

% Women of working age:-	1983-86	1987-91	1993-96	1997-00	2001-04	2005-08
Working	54	59	59	64	67	67
(Of whom – Full-time)	35	37	36	38	42	41
(Of whom – Part-time)	19	22	23	25	25	25
Inactive	12	12	14	14	14	15
Retired	1	1	1	2	2	2
Looking after home	33	28	26	20	17	16
Base total	3281	4570	5270	4280	4342	6511

The next table (1.6) shows that with growing participation rates there has been some polarisation in the types of work being done by women. Professional and responsible managerial jobs have increased. This reflects in small part the trajectory of work in the British economy generally. But also, and more to the point, it is a sign of the greater penetration by women into higher status sectors. Just as shown above for work *values*, this shift was most rapid in the early period covered here and has tailed off since the mid 1990s.

But this upgrading process does not reach down to lower level work. The growth in managerial and professional work has cut into

Intermediate occupations – mainly administrative and clerical – but not routine manual and service work. The figures given here in fact show manual work as increasing recently. But this is partly a technical effect, caused by revisions in 2001 to the Registrar-General's classificatory schema, which downgraded a number of jobs in which women figure prominently by redefining them as manual rather than intermediate. The likely overall position is that the proportion of female employment in manual occupations has remained broadly steady (though subject to increasing 'inactivity' through unemployment) while a growing proportion of those at non-manual levels (who are also the more likely to be actually working) are in professional jobs.

Table 1.6 Occupational class of women working age
(Pooled periods; rounded percentages)

% Women who are:-	1983-86	1987-91	1993-96	1997-00	2001-04	2005-08
Managerial/Professional	21	25	27	29	30	31
Intermediate	41	39	37	36	28	28
Routine/Manual workers	38	37	36	36	41	41
Base total	*3281*	*4570*	*5270*	*4280*	*4342*	*6511*

The factor of motherhood

Mothers and work

Within this general picture a variety of different patterns can be found, mainly according to whether or not a woman has children. These variations are extremely important, as they are pointers to the continuing centrality of the private realm in many women's lives. We will look here firstly just at the differences made by motherhood to women's behaviour and values, before going on to consider their meaning and implications.

To start with, we can see how motherhood relates to actual work behaviour. Tables 1.7, 1.8 and 1.9 set out the main differences between mothers and non-mothers in economic participation. Table 1.7 shows, for full-time working, how the growth in labour-force participation over this period has had more impact on mothers than non-mothers.

Table 1.7 Motherhood and work: a. Full-time
(Pooled periods; rounded percentages)

(Women Working Age)

% Working Full-time:-	1983-86	1987-91	1993-96	1997-00	2001-04	2005-08
All Childless	57	67	59	62	62	60
All Mothers	21	27	26	30	33	33
Mothers with child under 13	13	18	19	20	25	24
Mothers with child under 4	9	12	14	16	19	19
Base range	*492-1975*	*718-3383*	*841-3691*	*625-2969*	*785-3931*	*994-4600*

Women have long worked full-time before having children, or where they had none. At the end of the 1980s there was a surge in the proportion of childless women working fulltime, which was partly accounted for by a fall in those working part-time (see following table). But this rise was not sustained. There was a noticeable fall with the 1993 recession, and only slight (and tentative) recovery since then – perhaps complicated by the growing number of young women in further education. Mothers on the other hand gradually increased their work rate right through to the beginning of the twenty-first century, since when it has stabilised.

The picture for part-time working is given in table 1.8. This is favoured by many mothers as it leaves more time for family work. So rates are consistently higher for mothers than non-mothers. But whereas the rate for non-mothers has remained flat, for mothers it has crept up – with a proportional rate of increase which is considerably higher for younger mothers. Even for mothers, though, there has been a flattening out since the turn of the century, with slight *falls* in the most recent period.

Table 1.8 Motherhood and work: b. Part-time
(Pooled periods; rounded percentages)

(Women Working Age)

% Working Part-time:-	1983-86	1987-91	1993-96	1997-00	2001-04	2005-08
All Childless	11	6	11	11	10	12
All Mothers	25	27	28	32	31	31
Mothers with child under 13	23	26	28	34	35	34
Mothers with child under 4	10	17	22	26	30	28
Base range	*492-1975*	*718-3383*	*841-3691*	*625-2969*	*785-3931*	*994-4600*

Table 1.9 Motherhood and work: c. Looking after home
(Pooled periods; rounded percentages)

(Women Working Age)

% Looking after Home:-	1983-86	1987-91	1993-96	1997-00	2001-04	2005-08
All Childless	14	5	7	4	4	4
All Mothers	46	37	34	26	23	23
Mothers with child under 13	56	48	43	35	31	33
Mothers with child under 4	73	61	55	49	42	44
Base range	*492-1975*	*718-3383*	*841-3691*	*625-2969*	*785-3931*	*994-4600*

The softening of mothers' work participation rates in recent years is matched by a corresponding small increase in the number of younger mothers (but not of non-mothers) who report themselves as looking after the home (table 1.9). The proportion of mothers active in the labour market probably peaked around five years ago, and has dropped back since then.

All of this follows a general peaking of pro-work values some time in the 1990s. It is not easy however to understand or interpret women's economic activity without looking at their values, and this is particularly true of mothers.[16] So we should now look at how motherhood relates to *values*.

Mothers' values

There are clear variations in women's relative evaluations of domesticity and paid work, according to whether or not they are mothers and the age of their children. Five of the key attitude variables presented earlier are considered here in turn, in tables 1.10 to 1.14, to illustrate how responses to them are influenced by these factors.

Table 1.10 Motherhood and values: a

(All women) (Question not asked in 1986)

	1990	1994	1998	2002	2006
% agree that family life may suffer if women work FT					
All childless	35	26	10	25	27
All mothers	46	36	32	37	39
Mothers with dependent child	44	30	28	36	40
Mothers with child under four	43	30	21	28	37
Base range	*160-1261*	*54-498*	**-474*	*109-1072*	*108-915*

Note: Where base falls below 100, figure given in pale font. An asterisk in baseline means that the base is below 50.

As already indicated in table 1.2, the attitude examined in table 1.10 fell to a low point of agreement in 1998, since when it has recovered somewhat. But when we split women into those with children and those without, it is clear that being a mother is linked with stronger levels of agreement. And while support for this proposition did fall among mothers too, it stopped at a higher level.

An interesting detail here is that this fall in support among mothers was most marked among younger mothers.[17] That is, it went down to 32% at its lowest for all mothers – i.e. including those with grown-up children – while down to around 21% among mothers with the youngest children. This is presumably because during the 1990s the new enthusiasm for working was generally rather higher in younger cohorts of women than older. So there were contradictory impulses operating among younger mothers. As young women they were part of the most strongly pro-work faction; but as mothers they also remained (relatively) pro-domestic. Over the last decade these contrary effects seem to have resolved themselves in favour of domesticity, as younger mothers have experienced a strong rebound of domestic values. What seems likely is that as more mothers have actually come to work full-time, the traditional belief that this is harmful to family life has become reinforced by personal experience and observation.

This is not quite the same with the attitude dealt with in table 1.11. Here, departure from the traditional view that children suffer if mothers work was even stronger among young mothers than among non-mothers – perhaps because young mothers *wanted* to work, but could not do so while holding onto this particular belief.

However it has been the youngest category of mothers who have recently returned to this view most emphatically and decisively. There have been growing anxieties among mothers in Britain for some years now, about the effects of working on families and communities. The Conservative Party has drawn attention to 'Broken Britain', and a number of organisations have promoted debates on particular aspects of this – such as the report last year for the Children's Society and the Joseph Rowntree discussion paper.[18] Perhaps the traditional view on this, presented in table 1.11 and which is shown in table 1.1 as continuing a general decline right up to 2006, may now be on the point of wider revival.

Table 1.11 Motherhood and values: b

(All women) (Question not asked in 1986 or 1998)

% agree that if women work children suffer	1990	1994	1998	2002	2006
All childless	37	32		24	28
All mothers	44	35		34	31
Mothers with dependent child	39	26		29	26
Mothers with child under four	38	26		19	29
Base range	162-1262	55-499		109-1073	108-918

Note: Where base falls below 100, figure given in pale font.

The next two variables follow a slightly different trajectory.

Table 1.12 Motherhood and values: c

(All women) (Question not asked in 1986 or 1998)

% agree that being housewife as fulfilling as paid job	1990	1994	1998	2002	2006
All childless	39	41		41	42
All mothers	48	44		51	53
Mothers with dependent child	40	43		48	48
Mothers with child under four	39	42		52	53
Base range	92-1261	55-502		110-1075	108-921

Table 1.13 Motherhood and values: d

(All women)   (Question not asked in 1998)

% agree that most women want home and children	1986	1990	1994	1998	2002	2006
All childless	23	25	22		16	23
All mothers	34	27	24		24	33
Mothers with dependent child	23	17	20		17	29
Mothers with child under four	20	18	20		15	32
Base range	*76-651*	*162-1267*	*55-500*		*110-1068*	*108-919*

In 1.12, dealing with appreciation of the role of housewife, young mothers seem to have created a vanguard of a recovery for this value as early as the late 1990s – having before that been no more favourable towards it than non-mothers. Table 1.13 shows a similar but stronger effect. During the late 1980s and 1990s young mothers were the most sceptical of the view that women want a home and children. But in the latest round (2006) they are the ones to record the sharpest bounce back to traditional views. If they are the opinion leaders now, as they were before, then further shift back to tradition seems assured.

This effect is even more marked in the final variable in this set, in table 1.14. This last variable here is widely taken as the acid test for really traditional notions of domesticity and sex roles. The figures in table 1.14 show that in 1986, notwithstanding some overall variability, mothers of young children could be regarded as quite traditional. This is consistent with their economically dependent social position, and low participation in the work-force. However they rapidly dropped these views, and became the category of women *most* hostile to traditional sex roles – right through to 2002.

The indications from 2006 data are however that they are now (in spite of, or possibly because of, much higher participation in the work force) re-adopting these views nearly as quickly as they dropped them in the first place.

Table 1.14 Motherhood and values: e

(All women)

	1986	1990	1994	1998	2002	2006
% agree that men and women should have different roles						
All childless	39	18	18	9	11	9
All mothers	43	25	23	19	17	17
Mothers with dependent child	37	15	18	12	7	11
Mothers with child under four	40	13	13	3	2	17
Base range	*173-1447*	*162-1263*	*54-502*	**-478*	*109-1074*	*108-920*

Note: Where base falls below 100, figure given in pale font. Asterisk denotes base of less than 50.

Overall support for this very traditional value may now have bottomed out – a decade or so later than for some of the other traditional (but less extreme) views considered here.[19] And young mothers seem to be in the forefront of any revival, as they were when opinion was moving the other way. All of which suggests that some alienation does appear to be taking place among younger women from the world of paid work. Many young mothers now only work at all because of financial pressures.[20]

What can *not* be denied is that ostensibly there is some dissonance between their behaviour - which is still committed to work, although showing signs of having peaked a little while ago – and their values, which perhaps indicate that they would like to be living differently. Paid work and family values appear to be pulling in different directions. But these apparently competing forces may actually be compatible insofar as work is seen as a means to serve family interests rather than as an end in itself. And, for mothers at any rate, this does indeed seem to be the case.

Working for the family

In contemporary research, the rather simplistic approach [in which women's 'central life interest' is seen as having more of a focus on family life] *has long been transcended.* (Rosemary Crompton & Clare Lyonette, 2007)

I am the editor of ELLE now, and we recently surveyed more than 1,000 women turning 30 to ask them what they wanted out of life, fully expecting that they would mirror my generation and put careers as their main focus. They didn't. They said they wanted to be happy, married and have a family as much as they wanted career success. Actually, they wanted it more than success. (Lorraine Candy, 2009)

What the BSA data seems to suggest has happened is that women – and not least mothers – have increasingly incorporated paid work into their expected pattern of life. But this does not seem to mean that many have changed their priorities. Indeed the clear preference of mothers for part-time work does support very strongly a conclusion that work is valued by most mothers insofar as it fits in with family and community life and serves *those* purposes. As Catherine Hakim has put it,

> *Wage work is an extension of* [the modern housewife's] *homemaking role, not an alternative to it; she seeks additional family income whereas the career woman seeks personal development and personal fulfilment, competing on equal terms with men.*[21]

For most women, the public realm continues to be subordinate to the private.

The primary identity test

There are no questions that I can find in BSA which seem to address very directly this matter of the detailed relationship between work and family life, or their relative importance. One which gets close is the periodic question on reasons for working, which contains a response option 'To follow my career', which fairly unambiguously specifies that work is important for its own sake. Typically twice as many of the women without children endorse this option, that is around 45% of childless working age women compared with just over 20% of mothers. But even questions like this do not present a clear view of the interconnection of work with family; any such links can only come out in analysis.

It is, therefore, the indirect evidence which is most compelling – for example that given by questions on identity. Thus, in 2006 there was a question asking 'If you had to pick just one thing from this list to describe yourself – something that is important to you when you think of yourself – what would it be?' There were about twenty options listed, starting with 'Working class', 'Elderly', 'A woman/A man', and so on. Easily the most popular choice for women of working age was 'A mother', at 35%, followed by 'A woman' (about 20%), then 'A working person', 'Working class' and so on, all at under 10%. This I think tells us a great deal about how important family life still is for women now – notwithstanding the scorn of some commentators on this.[22]

We can categorise women according to their first choice responses to this question. All those giving priority to a family or kinship-based identity ('Mother', 'Wife' or 'Partner') can be grouped together as choosing a private identity. Those selecting something relating more to the world of work or politics ('A working person', 'Middle class', 'A woman' and so on) can be seen as selecting a universal or *public* identity.

Respondents grouped in this way show a definite pattern of values and behaviour, and even of happiness. Table 1.15 sets out some of this. Thus women selecting a private identity are clearly drawn to more positive evaluations of (traditional) domestic life than others. This does not mean that they are not working. Almost as many are, though they are more likely to be part-time. Most importantly, those who are working do seem to be more satisfied with their jobs than are those women whose focus is within the public domain.

25

Presumably, 'mothers' who regard employment mainly as a means to an end can be more relaxed at work than 'women' oriented to a career. To point this out is not to question the validity of careers for women: it is simply to draw attention to something that is too often ignored by policy-makers – that lack of a *career* does not generally matter to mothers in the way it would to non-mothers.

Table 1.15 Values associated with private and public identities
(Rounded percentages)

(Women working age)

VALUES: % agree/disagree with proposition		Private ID	Public ID
Man's job to earn money...	Agree	15	6
	Disagree	55	83
Being housewife rewarding as paid job..	Agree	59	43
	Disagree	18	31
Job OK but woman wants home/children..	Agree	32	22
	Disagree	36	55
Family life suffers if woman works FT...	Agree	37	31
	Disagree	45	55
ECONOMIC STATUS:			
	Working	61	75
	(Working full-time)	32	52
	(Working part-time)	28	23
	Looking after home	26	9
HAPPINESS:			
Very satisfied with job (if working)		43	34
Very satisfied with family life		65	58
Personally very happy		56	53
	Base totals	*541*	*570*

Source: BSA 2006

Table 1.16 explores the issue of happiness further. It is noteworthy from table 1.15 that women with primarily private identities are (a shade) happier personally, as well as in their family lives. What is likely to be the linking factor here is the valuing of domesticity. Table 1.16 shows that there is a direct relationship between agreeing that being a housewife can be fulfilling and both personal and family happiness.

Table 1.16 Levels of happiness by view on housewife role

(Row percentages)

(Women working age)

Agree/disagree that housewife role is as fulfilling as paid job	Satisfied with family life			Personally happy		
	Very	Fairly	Not	Very	Fairly	Not
Agree	65	28	7	56	35	9
Neither agree/disagree	61	30	9	45	42	13
Disagree	58	35	6	41	47	13

Bases: 300 Agree: 171 Neither agree/disagree: 174 Disagree   Source: BSA 2006

The significance of part-time working

There is no need actually to be a fulltime housewife in order to appreciate the positive nature of the role, and its place at the heart of local community life. It may indeed be the growing recognition of this, and a corresponding reinstatement of family and community life as central to society, rather than peripheral, which is prompting the shifts of attitudes and behaviour among young mothers currently. There is no inherent contradiction between valuing the housewife role and working – especially part-time. Part-time work is a well-tried means of reconciling a need or desire for paid work with an appreciation of the over-riding importance of family life.

Indeed, working part-time can of course also be conceptualised as being a part-time housewife! It is a working arrangement which allows women to participate in *both* social realms. Through it, when women become mothers they can stay part of the community of work, which in contemporary society is where they may need to be in order to feel within the mainstream. But they can also keep one foot very firmly in the private realm. So part-time working enables them to achieve a balance, which does appear to be more important to most than having an equal stake to men's in the public realm. What is very significant here is that women working part-time are not only happier in themselves and their family lives than those working full-time, but *also* than housewives not working at all.[23]

Table 1.17 Levels of happiness by time spent at work
(Row percentages)

(Women working age)

Economic status	Satisfied with family life			Personally happy		
	Very	Fairly	Not	Very	Fairly	Not
Working Full Time	63	33	5	54	37	9
Working Part Time	72	25	4	56	38	6

Bases: 262 Full-time: 168 Part-time   Source: BSA 2006

Unfortunately many analysts and commentators in this field have been reluctant to acknowledge this; and those like Catherine Hakim who have recognised women's attachment to domestic life – including the preference of many to look after their children themselves - have come under heavy attack. This issue will be examined more later on; but it is appropriate to end this first chapter with a brief discussion about the nature of this argument. What soon becomes clear from a perusal of the literature is that there is no real disagreement about the basic fact that many women, particularly mothers, choose to work part-time where this is available to them, and seem happy to do so. Many also choose to do their own childcare. All this has long been recognised in BSA's own commentaries on this topic, which were regular and frequent in the early years of the survey, and which constitute an influential chunk of the work done on it. Where there have been differences of opinion however is in the interpretation of this fact, and the drawing of implications.

Thus as early as the report on the 1986 survey, Sheena Ashford spelt out in some detail, and without criticism, the popularity of part-time working for mothers when children had started school and no longer needed constant care. It allowed a mother to combine some working with a reasonable amount of time at home.[24] The following year Sharon Witherspoon echoed that part-time work was favoured by women in the UK. She then pointed out how this hindered their promotion prospects and increased their economic disadvantage relative to men.[25] This point was then repeated by her in 1991:

> *Increasingly, however, there is doubt as to whether part-time working is, after all, such a panacea. In the first place, the move to part-time working after the birth of a child is often associated with downward occupational mobility, since higher-level jobs are not usually available on a part-time basis." And part-time pay rates are lower too.* [26]

A few years later, however, Katarina Thomson carried out a very thorough and sensitive analysis of why some women did not work at all. In almost all cases this was because they enjoyed being with their children, and felt that this was better for them anyway. Thomson concluded that "... whether or not mothers go out to work appears to be a social *choice* which reflects women's values about the role of women in work and the family." And no policymaker should try to do anything without recognising this.[27] But commentaries since then, as fewer mothers have stayed at home completely, have become openly hostile to housewifery and less sympathetic than formerly to part-time working, which Rosemary Crompton and Clare Lyonette have tried to damn by referring to as 'perpetuating a modified male-breadwinner role'.[28]

The culture war

The reason for this hostility seems to be that, in the eyes of commentators such as these, traditional family practices, even or especially *modified* traditional practices, are not connected to women's own desires, but are cultural inventions which constrain women into particular roles that are against their better interests. Crompton and most other academic commentators in this area do not seem to believe that any woman really wants to play a central part in family life – which they tend to dismiss as unwelcome 'conventionally assigned family responsibilities', which get thrust on women from outside.[29] These would *not* be chosen by free women who were allowed to exercise their own wills.

In a very revealing passage in their analysis, Crompton and Lyonette consider what theories exist for explaining why women have not made fuller use of available opportunities in the labour market.[30] Firstly they suggest that there are 'rational economic' models – in which men and women are interchangeable - arguing in terms of the most effective usage of family resources. Then there are 'gender construction' approaches, including their own, which look at the way that certain social roles 'get allocated to women'. Finally, they refer very briefly (and dismissively) to theories which argue from men and women's different natures, and the different interests and desires which they may develop as a result of these. Most significantly, they cannot bring themselves to present this last type as a *scientific* option like the previous two. They designate it instead as 'conventional morality', with all of the derogatory connotations that this phrase can conjure up. In this way they are able to discount such approaches, and are free to represent women as victims of external circumstances (such as 'working practices') and men's selfish construction of systems of roles which deprive women of all the best social opportunities, and require them to perform many of the most arduous tasks. Nowhere is there any recognition that some women (even a few) may derive any satisfaction from family life.

There is a place for this sort of approach. But if it is the only one that we can draw on then I feel that our understanding of what women want is bound to remain deficient. For if one thing shines out for me from the findings I have presented above it is that the recent shifts in attitudes demonstrated by younger mothers, which could represent the first stirrings of return to more traditional views in Britain, have all the appearance of a thoroughly *spontaneous* reaction, coming from deep inside them as individuals. I am not aware of any movements or groups who could be drumming up such responses. There is no *Women and Family Commission*. And it is precisely because of this that people like Lorraine Candy, quoted above, are so surprised when they discover what young women *do* feel.

It just does not seem plausible to attribute all this to a cultural construction of gender. It looks to me much more like a natural expression of *sex*, meaning those basic reproductive strategies which probably govern much more of our behaviour than we like to think.[31] Mothers are wired to respond to the needs of their offspring. And this is arguably what most will organise their lives around for as long as their children – and possibly their children's children too – need them to.[32] Mothers do not give priority to their children because 'society' or the state tells them to – nor other mothers, nor magazine editors, nor even male partners. They do it, I believe, because they feel driven from inside to do so, and feel happier when they *do*. In most societies this would be taken as too obvious to mention. In Britain it is currently dismissed by opinion leaders as outmoded conventional morality. So what may be happening now is that more young mothers are feeling the need to resist the imposition of a dominant, pro-work culture, which refuses to acknowledge fully their most powerful drives.

A mistake about work

If this argument is valid, it could raise some questions about how a 'pro-work culture' came to be adopted so enthusiastically by young mothers in the first place, a generation ago. The basic answer to this would be that this is not quite what happened. The revolution in values which the baby-boomers pioneered, and which underlies dominant attitudes today, was not a 'pro-work' movement as such. It was basically a 'pro-choice' revolution, which embraced working insofar as that was what women might want. The BSA data confirms this. Response options emphasising people's (especially women's) right to choose for themselves what they do are the ones that generally get the strongest support.

But this revolution may have changed its character after New Labour took up the cause of pro-choice values to attract the female vote. For once the party had gained power, its support for women's right to work shifted, perhaps inevitably, into support for *working* women rather than their right to choose. The right of women to work has subsequently become a duty; and it is this which I think conflicts with desires arising out of motherhood, in which a level of personal autonomy and self-management is always likely to figure quite powerfully. The reactions of women to this development have so far been individual and spontaneous. But if the government fails to recognise them and accommodate them, then they could quite easily become more collective and self-conscious. A counter-revolution is not out of the question. So there is a challenge for policymakers here. They urgently need to fact up to the fact that the values underlying much current social policy may not match the desires of women to the extent that they have assumed.

At the moment government seems to think that women need supports which protect and relieve them from family obligations. But that is almost certainly a misunderstanding, arising perhaps from an assumption that women want to be like men and will do so if given a decent chance. To back this up a little, and as the final detail here, I add a small table showing how support among mothers for action on equal opportunities seems to be weakening. Table 1.18 looks at the age distribution of the view that equality legislation to protect the rights of women in the labour market has not yet gone far enough. There is a definite lessening of resolution among younger mothers, which is consistent with the revival shown above in women's appreciation of the importance of the private realm of family and community life.

Table 1.18   Mothers' support for equal opportunities, by age

(All mothers)

Age of mother	18-34	35-49	50-64	65+
% agreeing that EO has not gone far enough	31	43	46	47
Bases	*223*	*382*	*373*	*370*

Source: BSA 2006

Conclusion and implications

BSA data provide us with some very useful instruments for improving our understanding of the growth of women's involvement in the labour market. What they show is that many more women are indeed working than twenty years ago – and that (as part of this) women spend more of their lives in the work-force. Also motherhood is no bar to work.

But this does not wipe out mothers' deeper interest in family and community life. There is a strong and reviving recognition of the value and appeal of the housewife role; and mothers who are able to spend at least part of their day looking after the home and children are more content with their lives than those who work fulltime.

So it is a mistake to assume that paid work has the same meaning for women as it does for men. Although there are no BSA questions directly covering this point, it seems likely that increasing numbers of women now feel (as most used to) that although they can and do make an important direct contribution to the national economy, this may not be as vital and fundamental as the part women play (and which men, as the non-reproducing sex, cannot) in running families and the informal community.

A likely corollary of this is that most women do value having a male breadwinner around. Implicit in the idea of women working part-time is that *men* in the family will be working full-time. Most women are looking for balance in their lives, and ways of maximising the wellbeing of their children, rather than the chance to dispense with men. I suspect that few do actually support policies which prioritise getting women into work where this is at the expense of male roles and motivation. Most want a hard-working male partner to bear the main economic burden for the family, and perform those functions they don't have the time or inclination to carry out themselves.

Unfortunately there are no BSA questions which deal directly with these issues. So we are reliant on indirect indicators. And that is what I shall look at in the next chapter, which considers where male partners stand in the eyes of contemporary British women.

CHAPTER 2   THE VALUE OF A MALE PARTNER

Rise of the independent mother

Growth in the numbers of working women has coincided with significant changes in relationships with men and the nature of domestic partnerships. The period covered by this analysis has seen a large increase in the number of women bringing up children without a male partner; and this second chaper considers some aspects of this and asks to what extent, and in what ways, this is something that many women actually want to be doing.

The division of economic labour

At the heart of this topic is a weakening in the traditional interdependence between men and women, whereby a woman wanting to raise children derived her major economic support from a long-term male partner, her husband. In their turn men would find much of their purpose in life, and position as useful members of the community, from providing a mother with this support.[1] Our first table here looks at the working rate of women and of their male partners, where they have one, across our sequence of key years.

Table 2.1 Economic activity of women and their male partners
(Key years; column percentages)

(Working age women)

Economic activity rates	1986	1990	1994	1998	2002	2006
WOMEN						
Working full-time	36	38	36	38	43	41
Working part-time	21	21	24	29	24	24
Not working	43	42	40	33	32	35

MALE PARTNERS						
Working full-time	62	62	57	56	54	52
Working part-time	1	1	2	2	2	3
Not working	11	10	11	11	10	10
No male partner	27	27	31	31	34	34
Bases	606	1131	1315	1226	1312	1632

The pattern is simple. There was a sustained increase in the overall number of women working during the period through to 2002, with a slight drop since. The has been accompanied by a considerable and continuing decline in the number of male partners who are working, and a corresponding increase in the numbers of women living *without* a partner.

These data become even more illuminating when the two measures – that is of women's own activity, and that of their partners – are combined to create a single measure showing the nature of their division of economic labour. A six-category schema is developed here for this purpose, containing the following categories. A 'Traditional' division of labour denotes households where the female respondent is not working, and her male partner is. 'Neo-conventional' refers to cases in which the man is working full-time, and the woman part-time. 'Egalitarian' households are where both are working equally – whether full or part-time. 'Reverse SDL' is where the woman is working more than her partner; and 'No-work couple' means that neither of them is in work. Choice of these working arrangements is strongly influenced by whether or not there are any children. So for the next table, showing changes in the distribution of these categories, mothers and women without children are separated.

Table 2.2 indicates that working arrangements for childless women have scarcely changed over the past twenty years. Where these women do have male domestic partners, which itself has been a fairly constant proportion, their division of labour in the public realm is essentially egalitarian. And insofar as their male partners do work more than the respondents themselves, this has been shifting from mainly a traditional mode to neo-conventional.

Table 2.2   Motherhood and the division of economic labour
(Key years; column percentages)

(Working age women)

Type of arrangement	1986	1990	1994	1998	2002	2006
WOMEN NO CHILDREN						
Traditional	7	5	6	5	5	4
Neo-conventional	2	3	6	4	5	6
Egalitarian	30	27	30	28	29	27
Reverse SDL	6	3	2	3	2	3
No-work couple	0	4	5	3	2	3
No Partner	56	59	52	57	58	57
Bases	*131*	*313*	*380*	*333*	*389*	*470*
MOTHERS						
Traditional	31	31	24	19	16	19
Neo-conventional	21	23	23	26	24	22
Egalitarian	19	20	19	20	23	21
Reverse SDL	5	3	4	8	6	6
No-work couple	9	8	9	7	8	7
No Partner	14	16	21	21	23	24
Bases	*475*	*818*	*935*	*892*	*922*	*1161*

These last two models seem to have more appeal for mothers, and the egalitarian somewhat less. This is presumably because mothers are more in need of the type of support which they give. For some time it looked as though the neo-conventional arrangement was taking over from the traditional as the mainstream model. Catherine

Hakim wrote in 1996;

> *By the 1990s in the western world the complete division of labour,*
> *which had encouraged wives to refrain altogether from*
> *employment outside the home, had been replaced by what we have*
> *called the modern family division of labour which allows the*
> *modern housewife to engage in employment that is subordinate to*
> *her domestic responsibilities, either part-time and/or part-year*
> *work or a job that is less demanding than her husband's.*[2]

But the recent signs of revival in more full-blooded traditionalism
puts the two arrangements on a more equal footing at the moment.
In any case, the main story for mothers over this period is the way in
which *traditional* partnerships have been overtaken by women living
without a male partner. These are in fact the only two categories to
register any real change.

Table 2.3 looks in more detail at the distribution of *traditional*
divisions of labour.

Table 2.3   Motherhood and the traditional division of labour
(Key years; column percentages)

% practicing traditional d.o.l.	1986	1990	1994	1998	2002	2006
WOMAN'S CIRCUMSTANCES						
[No children]	7	5	6	5	5	4
All mothers	31	31	24	19	16	19
Mother with dependent child	36	36	28	21	20	21
Mother with dependent child under 13	41	41	30	22	22	23
Mother with dependent child under four	54	54	33	32	26	29
Base range	*193-463*	*179-773*	*201-943*	*177-908*	*128-629*	*243-1074*

Again, it is mothers of the youngest children who are particularly interesting. It is when children are of pre-school (and even pre-nursery) age that mothers are least keen to work, and most durably to appreciate the benefits of a male breadwinner. That does indeed emerge from the data when it is tabulated according to the age of a mother's youngest child. The rate of 'traditional' partnerships is higher, and has *remained* higher even as this type of arrangement has become generally less popular, the younger and more dependent that a mother's children are.

But the main story here, it must be emphasised, has to be the replacement of these traditional partnerships by mothers living without any partner at all.

Focussing on single mothers

As the proportion of mothers without a male partner has risen, so too there seem to have been several shifts in their demographic and social characteristics. But before we can look at these properly we need to establish what exactly we mean by single motherhood.[3]

There is no universally-agreed definition of what constitutes lone motherhood. For the administration of social services there is a concept of lone mother households as benefit units, consisting of adult women living with dependent children. But this is too narrow for analytic purposes, in at least two main respects. In the first place it fails to allow for the fact that mothers do not cease mothering when their children happen to become full citizens themselves. Motherhood is for ever: and some of its most demanding stages do not really get underway until children start to function as adults themselves.[4] Secondly the benefit unit concept of lone mother embraces widows, who do not share many of the problems commonly associated with single mothers. Several of the prominent features of lone mothers' lives are bound up with limited access to their children's *paternal* relatives. But this seldom applies to widows. When a man who is in an established relationship dies, his parents and siblings usually lavish additional attention on his widow and children, not less. So the social life of widows tends to be very different from that of mothers where there is no relationship with a father, or only one that is broken and bitter.

So for our purposes here and in subsequent chapters, single mothers have been defined as those not widows, andwho are not living with a male partner. Of course, even this notion has is limitations. For example, there are many mothers these days who, for a variety of reasons (including the need to maximise welfare benefits) have more-or-less-steady male partners with whom they do not actually live. It falls within the concept of LAT – living apart while 'together'. Researchers encounter a lot of this on the ground.[5] But precisely because such mothers are, in the nature of things, likely to be avoiding official attention it is virtually impossible to identify them in survey data and to estimate how many of them there are. Even if we did want to separate them out in the BSA data, we could not do so.[6]

But we do need to bear them in mind, all the time, because there is a lot of overlap between lone mothers and those with partners. Single mothers are not a different species. Indeed, many authorities and commentators prefer to think of lone motherhood as a stage through which many women may pass briefly, and which only relatively few may spend a long time in. *Gingerbread* publicises around five-and-a-half years as the average duration of such a stage currently.[7] But as their notion of being a lone mother seems to terminate automatically when children are no longer dependent I would be cautious about adopting that figure for analytic purposes.

Having spelt out these reservations and qualifications, it is possible to start examining some basic characteristics of single mothers in the BSA data. The first and most self-evident aspect is that their numbers, or rather the proportions of all women and mothers that they represent, have been steadily growing, although with some flattening out in recent years. Table 2.4 summarises the data here, using the four-year blocs of pooled survey materials in order to smooth out minor fluctuations.

The first two measures here relate to single mothers as proportions of the female population, rather than of mothers as such. The majority of women are mothers by the age of 35; but some remain childless into old age. So the proportions of single mothers in the first two rows of the table are bound to be smaller than for those dealing with mothers. But they do nevertheless show steady growth over the period of analysis. This increase is partly due to the growing proportion of mothers spending some time single; but it also reflects the aging process. There were few single mothers before the 1970s. But by the 1990s, as later tables will confirm, those pioneers who had not subsequently settled with a partner were moving into mid-life cohorts which had not previously contained single mothers apart from widows. The proportions of lone mothers among working age women are higher than those among all women, because the latter group contains older cohorts, which relatively few single mothers have yet reached.

Table 2.4   Single mothers as proportions of all women/mothers
(4-year pooled; column %)

Single Mothers as % of:-	1983-86	1987-91	1993-96	1997-00	2001-04	2005-08
All women	*	8	11	12	14	15
Working age women	*	10	13	14	16	17
Mothers with dep.t children	10	13	19	23	24	25
Mothers with children under 13	9	14	20	23	23	25
Mothers with children under 4	5	15	19	20	19	21
Bases	*492-4486*	*718-6321*	*841-7798*	*625-6326*	*785-8059*	*994-9608*

* It is not possible to identify respondents with *adult* children reliably until 1987.

The remaining three rows in the table deal with mothers at different points in their motherhood careers. Those whose children include under-fours are at an earlier point than those who only have older dependent children. Mothers who only have *older* children generally contain a higher proportion who are single, simply because many single mothers start out in a couple and then become single at some later point. So the proportion at this later stage is cumulative. Mothers who are single with very young children, on the other hand, are more likely to have been alone from the outset, at the child's birth. So their rate of singularity is not cumulative. On the contrary, it requires constant replenishment from more 'always alone' mothers.

It is therefore interesting to notice in this table the changing gradients of proportions across the three rows. In 1983-6 there were relatively few single mothers among the mothers of younger children, compared with the older. The resulting slope (5% among youngest, up to 10% among oldest) would suggest that the main source of single motherhood at this time was the breakdown of relationships – leading to a build-up of single motherhood in later stages of parenting. Then in 1987-91 there was a dramatic jump in the proportion of single mothers of younger children to a level where the slope went the other way (down from 15% for mothers of children under four to 13% of the *oldest* category). This is a strong indicator that lifestyle single motherhood had suddenly grown in popularity during the late 1980s, with more women having their children without going through a period of co-habitation first. This interpretation is corroborated by other data which is presented later.

The later periods in table 2.4 document gentler increases in single motherhood, with the gradient between these three rows levelling out and even swinging back a little the other way again. This in its turn suggests that while there are still many 'never-together' single mothers joining the system (otherwise the percentages in the bottom row would drop right down again) the pace of *increase* of single motherhood may now be moderating.

Characteristics of single mothers

This pattern is consistent with the age-structure of single mothers, which is explored in tables 2.5 and 2.6.

From table 2.5 it is clear how single-motherhood is gradually percolating into older generations. It will however be some time before the distribution matches that of mothers with partners.

Indeed, for as long as some single mothers do continue to settle with male partners at some point, parity is unlikely to be achieved.

Table 2.5   Ages of single and other mothers.
(4-year pooled; column %)

(All women)   (No reliable data before 1987)

Age of mother	1983-86	1987-91	1993-96	1997-00	2001-04	2005-08
SINGLE MOTHERS						
18-34	*	44	42	34	26	26
35-49	*	31	33	36	41	38
50-64	*	19	19	22	24	24
65+	*	8	8	8	10	14
MOTHERS WITH PARTNERS						
18-34	*	20	20	17	15	14
35-49	*	34	35	33	32	30
50-64	*	25	23	26	29	27
65+	*	21	22	24	24	29
Bases: SM		*622*	*1199*	*1085*	*1530*	*2012*
MWP		*5699*	*6599*	*5241*	*6529*	*7596*

Table 2.6 illustrates how the age patterns among mothers of young children are already quite similar for single and partnered mothers. But they may not get much closer. For whereas partnered mothers are steadily getting older, with a decline in the proportion under 25, and increase in those 45 or over, the youngest category of single mothers is somewhat larger and already appears to be growing again. If single-motherhood has become a stage in life that many women go through *before* finding a partner, then this differential seems unlikely ever to go away.

Table 2.6   Age of mothers of younger children
(4-year pooled; column %)

(Mothers with dependent children up to 12)

Age of mother	1983-86	1987-91	1993-96	1997-00	2001-04	2005-08
SINGLE MOTHERS						
18-24	18	24	16	18	12	20
25-34	49	52	51	45	40	34
35-44	28	21	27	33	40	38
45+	5	3	6	4	8	7
MOTHERS WITH PARTNERS						
18-24	11	8	6	6	6	7
25-34	48	48	48	44	39	35
35-44	37	39	39	43	47	48
45+	4	5	7	7	9	10
Bases: SM	*109*	*303*	*643*	*522*	*724*	*808*
MWP	*830*	*994*	*1372*	*1086*	*1247*	*1457*

A similar conclusion can be drawn from an examination of trends in the marital/domestic status of single mothers. This is dealt with in tables 2.7 and 2.8.

Since the mid 1980s there has been a rapid decline in the incidence of marriage among working age women generally, with corresponding rises in cohabitation, never having lived with a male partner and, to a lesser extent, divorce and separation. See table 2.7.

Table 2.7 Marital/domestic status of working age women.[8]

(4-year pooled; column %)

(Working Age Women) (See note 2.8 on pages 146-7)

% women reporting selves as:-	1983-86	1987-91	1993-96	1997-00	2001-04	2005-08
Married	70	67	60	56	53	50
Co-habiting/living as married	3	6	9	11	12	13
Separated/divorced	7	7	10	11	11	11
Widowed	3	2	2	2	2	2
Never married or cohabiting	16	18	19	20	22	24
Bases	*3281*	*4570*	*5270*	*4280*	*4342*	*6511*

Table 2.8 Marital/domestic status of single mothers

(Key years; column %)

(See note 2.8 on pages 146-7)

% single mothers reporting selves as:-	1986	1990	1994	1998	2002	2006
ALL WORKING-AGE:						
Separated/divorced	78	79	65	61	60	52
Never married or co-habiting	18	20	30	34	38	38
Other (Married/co-hab)	2	2	4	5	3	10
WITH CHILD UNDER 13:						
Separated/divorced	83	57	59	49	46	40
Never married or cohabiting	15	41	38	46	50	57
Other (Married/co-hab)	2	2	3	4	4	3
Bases - Working age	*60*	*94*	*182*	*174*	*189*	*247*
Child under 13	***	*69*	*164*	*145*	*155*	*187*

Note: Where base falls below 100, figure given in pale font. Asterisk denotes base under 50.

As shown in table 2.8, among single mothers the rise in never having had a partner appears to be much greater. This also entails a drop in the proportion who have had partners but are now divorced or separated. For those single mothers with younger children, twelve or under, this transformation has some years ago passed the point at which those who have never lived with a partner may outnumber those who once did. Sample bases in the lower half of table 2.8 are rather small for some of these (early) years. But the changes portrayed since 1986 are so great that the general nature of the shift is now hard to doubt. The jump in the bottom row from 15% in 1986 to 41% in 1990 is particularly striking. But it does tally with the findings in the bottom row of table 2.4, which suggested from the overall distribution of single motherhood that a surge must be taking place in the 'never together' type. So it does seem likely that remarkable, and rapid, transitions were actually taking place then.

Lone mothers at work

To sum up the analysis so far, in the 1980s single mothers were mainly women whose lives had been affected by separation and divorce. But since then their ranks have been swollen increasingly by women who have in some degree chosen to become mothers without or before going through marriage or cohabitation. This shift seems likely to have a number of implications for mothers' social attitudes and, above all, economic behaviour. This is what we turn to now.

Levels of working

For baby boomers, in the early years of the libertarian shift, being a single mother often implied a strong commitment to work, and a desire to be an independent person through a paid job when a relationship with a male partner broke down. But this assumption does not fit the pattern of behaviour and attitudes we find emerging over the last two decades. Since the mid 1980s, the rates of economic activity of mothers have climbed. But when we split single mothers from those with partners it is evident that this is rather *more* true of mothers with partners than of lone mothers. Table 2.9 considers two age/family stage groups, that is all mothers with dependent children and those who have a child up to the age of twelve.

Table 2.9 Work with and without male partner
(4-year pooled; column %)

(Categories of mothers)

% working	1983-86	1987-91	1993-96	1997-00	2001-04	2005-08
SINGLE MOTHERS						
Mothers with dependent children	38	40	34	45	54	50
Mothers with dependent children under 13	28	36	29	38	45	44
MOTHERS WITH PARTNERS						
Mothers with dependent children	44	51	55	62	66	66
Mothers with dependent children under 13	36	46	53	58	64	63
Base ranges – SM	*109-154*	*303-377*	*643-741*	*522-636*	*724-812*	*808-1040*
MWP	*830-1132*	*994-1393*	*1372-1690*	*1086-1236*	*1247-1442*	*1457-1813*

From this table it is clear that having a partner, and no children under thirteen, offers the best circumstances for managing a job; this is the category of mothers here with the highest rates of work throughout the period covered. Likewise, *having* children under thirteen, and *no* partner, constitutes the most difficult domestic environment for working of those considered here; and this is where the lowest rates are found.

But between these extremes there are no obvious rules. At the outset of BSA surveys, having young children seems to have been the more limiting factor, and single mothers with only older children had a higher probability of working than those with partners but younger children. The expansion of childcare facilities plus a rapid change in childrearing culture seem to have tackled that restriction quite quickly though. By the early 1990s the number of mothers of younger children who were working had shot up. Since then it has been single motherhood itself which has provided the major obstacle to work.

Rates of work for all mothers with partners have risen steadily, with merely a small falling back over the most recent period. The progress of single mothers has however been hesitant and subject to setbacks. They were much more heavily affected by the 1993 recession, and also have reduced their participation again in the last 4-year period, much more seriously than mothers with partners. There are probably a number of interacting reasons for this – ranging from the greater practical obstacles they face, which would make it necessary to find greater motivation, to their readier access to benefits when not working, which would of course help to *weaken* that motivation. It would be ironic if there were also some more fundamental predisposition of single mothers towards domestic life. Government efforts to get women generally into the workforce sometimes look as if their real objective has been specifically to get single mothers off benefits. That is, if 'women' as a whole increase their economic activity, single mothers would get pulled in too, without the government appearing to lean on them. Insofar as that is what underlies the drive to get women working, then so far it has been a resounding failure.

This differential in activity rates is paralleled by a status difference in work done. Single mothers tend to be engaged in relatively low status, less responsible jobs. Again there are a variety of possible factors underlying this, from the consequences of simply having longer periods of inactivity (making it harder to pursue a career) to a (self-perpetuating) lesser commitment to work because of limited rewards available. Table 2.10 illustrates the resulting gap between single mothers and others, using data relating to mothers of younger children as this is where the difference between the two types of mother is greatest.

The bulk of work done by single mothers seems always to have been routine, manual work. But it is perhaps noteworthy that the amount of higher status work done by them has increased steadily, at the expense of intermediate occupations. This is a pointer towards a way in which single motherhood may be diverging at the moment, with a sharpening of the division between those who have careers (and are much more likely to be actually working, and doing so full-time) and those who can only get poorly paid work. These are more likely to be inactive and living on benefits. The latter are also the larger group, and growing; and their expansion has perhaps been an important factor behind the change in values which is evident among single mothers in recent years.

Table 2.10 Class/status of mothers' occupations
(4-year pooled; column %)

(Mothers with dependent children under 13)

	1983-86	1987-91	1993-96	1997-00	2001-04	2005-08
SINGLE MOTHERS						
Managerial/Professional	9	14	15	19	16	19
Intermediate	40	38	34	29	27	25
Routine/Manual workers	51	48	51	52	57	56
MOTHERS WITH PARTNERS						
Managerial/Professional	21	23	27	28	31	34
Intermediate	37	39	38	35	31	29
Routine/Manual workers	42	38	35	37	39	37
Bases - SM	*109*	*303*	*643*	*522*	*724*	*808*
MWP	*830*	*994*	*1372*	*1086*	*1247*	*1457*

Single mothers' attitudes towards work

Many BSA variables indicate that a definite shift of attitudes *away* from valuing work has been taking place among single mothers, both absolutely and relative to other categories of women. It has to be noted however that the change vis-à-vis other groups of women may come down in large part to age. As we have seen, single mothers tend to be younger than other mothers; and just as in the early years of BSA it was younger women who led the movement in favour of work, so younger women now are leading the return to domesticity. Unfortunately we cannot control for this properly in analyses, as the numbers of single mothers are too small to allow for very detailed break-downs. So it needs always to be borne in mind. Having noted this, it can be said that some of the tabulations which follow here do reveal quite strong differences, suggesting that single mothers almost certainly have shifted their priorities more than other women of the same age.

Responses to a BSA question in 1986 show that at that time single mothers had even stronger belief in the world of work than women without children – also a predominantly young group. This is shown in table 2.11.

Table 2.11   Views on best economic division of labour
(1986; row %)

(Working Age Women categories)

Preferred arrangement % responses of:	For a family with children under 5 years old, which arrangement is best?			For a family with children in their early teens, which arrangement is best?		
	Trad.	NC	Egal or RR	Trad.	NC	Egal or RR
Women no children	73	22	5	13	64	23
Single mothers	69	21	10	13	61	26
Mothers with partners	82	17	2	18	69	13

Bases: Women no children 124: Single mothers 66: Mothers with partners 381.
Abbreviations of arrangements: Trad. – traditional, NC – neo-conventional, Egal – egalitarian, RR – role reversal. See table 2.2, above, for definitions.

Answers elicited by another question, run in 1989 and then again in

1997 show how single mothers may have moved from being highly pro-work in the late eighties to a more moderate position by the mid/late nineties. (See table 2.12.)

Table 2.12   Views on importance of working
(1989 & 1997; row %)

(Working Age Women)

	1989	1997	Bases
% **agreeing** 'Work is a person's most important activity'			
Women no children	25	25	121-235
Single mothers	37	22	*- 78
Mothers with partners	30	15	141-359

In 1994 single mothers were still less domestic in orientation than other mothers, as indicated by answers (given in table 2.13) to a question asking *non*-working mothers *why* they did not work.

Table 2.13   Importance of reasons for not working
(1994; row %)

(Working Age Women: Mothers not working)

Importance of that reason	I enjoy spending time with my children more than working				It's better for the children if I am home to look after them			
	Very	Fairly	Not	n/a	Very	Fairly	Not	n/a
Single mothers	57	31	9	3	54	40	3	3
Mothers with partners	71	23	3	2	74	22	2	2

Bases: Single mothers   60: Mothers with partners   115.

All these findings tally with answers (table 2.14) from the running question on when women should work, which was introduced earlier in table 1.3.

Table 2.14 Women's views on working when there is pre-school child
(Key years: column %)

(% of All women)   (Question not asked in 1986 and 1998)

	1986	1990	1994	1998	2002	2006
% responses to question 'Do you think that women should work outside the home full-time, part-time or not at all when there is a child under school age?'						
WOMEN WITH NO CHILDREN:						
Work full-time		6	6		6	3
Work part-time		32	31		42	38
Stay home		50	46		37	32
Don't know/n.a.		12	17		15	26
Base		*395*	*636*		*489*	*573*
SINGLE MOTHERS:						
Work full-time		7	10		3	0
Work part-time		37	31		36	39
Stay home		46	46		43	40
Don't know/n.a.		6	14		18	21
Base		*143*	*303*		*364*	*476*
MOTHERS WITH PARTNERS:						
Work full-time		3	5		3	3
Work part-time		28	33		34	40
Stay home		61	54		50	39
Don't know/n.a.		7	8		13	18
Base		*1003*	*1018*		*1035*	*1322*

Relative both to women without children and mothers with partners, single mothers show here a lesser belief in the importance of full-time working, a relatively steady advocacy of *part*-time work and a much firmer attachment to the idea that mothers with pre-school children should not work at all outside the home. That is, by comparison with these two other categories of women, they show a drift from pro-work to domestic values over this period. This is consistent with the shifts of opinion manifested by young mothers in recent years on a wide range of related issues.

Social attitudes of single mothers

Single mothers are in the vanguard of change on all those attitudes we have explored here which suggest the beginning of possible revival in the 'private realm'. Unfortunately, as mentioned a little earlier, there are not enough cases for us to be able to unscramble the factors underlying this. Single mothers are heavily represented among the very youngest category of mothers. It is not possible to determine how much of the single mother effect should be attributed simply to their age, and how much to other characteristics. There is little that can be done about this, because the same attitude questions are not asked every year – so that answers cannot be pooled to increase sample size – and even when they *are* fielded they are only given to a sub-section of the annual sample. But this does not mean that these findings are not worth analysing. Being young is integral to what single motherhood has been all about. So it is not a disaster if the specific effect of age as such cannot be isolated through precise analysis. The data are still valuable, even if mainly as descriptive evidence. The next table (2.15) shows what happens to the 'work versus domesticity' measures when single mothers and mothers with partners are separated.

These figures confirm how well established the shift among single mothers to prioritising domestic concerns now is. On sex roles, single mothers moved further away from traditional views in the 1990s, but have been staging a modest recovery for at least six years now – while mothers generally (pulled in particular by middle aged baby boomers) are still easing away from them. It is the same with views about the effects on children of mothers working. For the 'women want a home' variable, single mothers were the first to show a revival of domesticity; but other mothers are not far behind and fast catching up. While for the housewife role question it is the other mothers who are leading the way back – having not departed nearly so far in the first place.

Table 2.15 Changing orientations to work and family
(Key years; column %)

(All women)

% agreeing that	1986	1990	1994	1998	2002	2006
Man's job to earn money*						
Single mothers	27	18	16	13	15	19
Mothers with partner	35	26	24	20	17	16
Children suffer if women work						
Single mothers		39	26		34	34
Mothers with partner		45	37		34	30
Women want home & family						
Single mothers	36	24	19		28	35
Mothers with partner	34	25	25		24	33
Being housewife rewarding						
Single mothers		38	28		47	50
Mothers with partner		49	45		51	54
Bases SM	*	*101*	*113*	*152*	*181*	*159*
MWP	*288*	*335*	*341*	*606*	*517*	*447*

* For this variable in this table, '1986' = 1984.

On balance, then, single mothers were clearly no less traditional than others in their views on work and family life in 2006, and arguably more so. So it is useful to be able to examine how this fits in with their ideas on a number of other issues bordering on the work-family heartland. Fortunately, in 2006 the number of single mothers in the

BSA sample is large enough to allow us to exclude older women (among whom single mothers are under-represented) and concentrate on more strictly comparable groupings – that is within the category of mothers with dependent children. The following batch of tables (2.16 to 2.18) look at the responses of these mothers in three overlapping areas; firstly issues relating directly to single parenthood itself, secondly to matters of financial support, and thirdly to assessments of the institution of marriage.

Endorsement of single parenting

Where single mothers do have very distinctive views, and not surprisingly, is in the assessment of the viability and desirability of single parenting itself. Table 2.16 collects some of the relevant measures together.

Table 2.16   Mothers' views on single parenting
(2006; row %)

(Mothers with dependent children: % who agree/disagree)

	Agree	Neither/ DK	Disagree	Base
One parent can bring up a child as well as two				
Single mothers	71	11	17	*165*
Mothers with partner	40	15	45	*546*
Don't need partner 2B happy/fulfilled				
Single mothers	84	8	7	*163*
Mothers with partner	68	20	11	*532*
Nothing wrong with a woman alone having child if she wants				
Single mothers	66	18	15	*165*
Mothers with partner	44	22	34	*546*
Relationships stronger when both partners are independent				
Single mothers	69	8	21	*162*
Mothers with partner	46	20	33	*530*

Most of this table should be self-explanatory. But the last item needs some comment. It derives from a BSA question relating to LAT, living apart but together, rather than about single parenting itself. But the positive response of single parents to it helps to underline that many of them do have *non-resident* partners. 34% of the single mothers with dependent children sampled in 2006 reported that they had such partners.

Table 2.17 Matters relating to financial support

(2006; row %)

(Mothers with dependent children)

% responding that:- Maintenance should depend on mother's income	Yes	DK	No	*Base*
Single mothers	53		47	*202*
Mothers with partner	76		23	*614*
Gov. should provide jobs if wants people to work				
Single mothers	63		38	*51*
Mothers with partner	40	9	49	*171*
Gov. responsible for decent living for unemployed				
Single mothers	71		29	*51*
Mothers with partner	37	9	53	*171*

RESPONDENT'S MAIN SOURCE OF INCOME	Own or spouse work		Benefits	
Single mothers	48		49	*210*
Mothers with partner	91		9	*714*

RESPONDENT'S ATTITUDE TO WELFARE STATE*	Symp.**	Average	Hostile	
Single mothers	44	41	14	*163*
Mothers with partner	31	42	27	*532*

* BSA 'welfarism' index, re-grouped into three categories
** = 'Sympathetic'

Table 2.17 illuminates just how far apart single and other mothers are on matters of financial support. Many single mothers are keen to avoid financial responsibilities, and proportionately more of them believe that levels of maintenance payments by fathers should not be influenced by mothers' earnings. This feeling extends to political views, where they consider that the government is responsible for the standard of living of all unemployed, and even for providing jobs. These feelings are linked with a sympathetic attitude towards the welfare state generally, together with a much higher reliance than other mothers on state benefits for their main income.

These positions diverge considerably from those of other mothers. And there is something distinctly traditional about them. They go against any notion that mothers should concern themselves with material providing. That is the job of fathers; or, in the absence of resident or supportive fathers, of what some feminists used to refer to (when the public domain was more of a male domain) as the 'patriarchal state'.[9]

Single mothers' views on marriage (table 2.18) ostensibly differ a good deal from those of other mothers. But this does not mean that they are hostile to marriage. In fact if their views are looked at carefully most of the differences can be seen to reflect doubts over whether marriage is currently a realistic option, more than a fundamental rejection of marriage as an ideal. Even the first proposition here, 'marriage is the best kind of relationship', is clearly referring to its standing in current social conditions. The last, 'marriage is a big risk', may go to the heart of the matter.

The responses of single mothers to this question suggest wariness. If they could rely on marriage working properly, many of them would be happy to try it. (Many of course will one day!) What makes them different to those mothers who do get married lies not in *wanting* to be alone and independent so much as in trying to *avoid* ending up alone against their will.[10] They value the marital ideal too *highly* for that. This is just part of what, on examination, appears to be a very traditional orientation.

Table 2.18   Mothers' views on marriage
(2006; row %)

(Mothers with dependent children)

% who	Agree	Neither/ DK	Disagree	Base
Marriage is the the best kind of relationship				
Single mothers	31	22	46	*165*
Mothers with partner	47	27	24	*546*
Marriage gives more financial security				
Single mothers	43	27	30	*165*
Mothers with partner	53	27	19	*546*
Marriage is only a piece of paper				
Single mothers	19	35	46	*165*
Mothers with partner	8	24	68	*546*
Many people stay in unhappy relationships because of money or children				
Single mothers	84	6	8	*165*
Mothers with partner	68	14	17	*546*
Given the divorce rate, getting married these days is a big risk				
Single mothers	49	31	19	*165*
Mothers with partner	23	34	42	*546*

What single mothers want

[Lone parent families] *represent* [in one sense] *the logical extreme of 'traditional' gender roles: women take almost total responsibility for the direct care of the children, and the father's role, if he is present at all, tends to be severely limited.* (Jacqueline Scott *et al*, 1994,)

It is conventional in British society to regard single mothers as work-orientated, and as needing public help precisely because of their difficulties in combining work and motherhood. But the more closely I have examined the data, the more I feel that this is surely a misperception. Most single mothers are very traditional *as* mothers. Where they now have a problem lies essentially in the fact that the operation of the benefit system discourages them from settling down with a male partner and using his parenthood to help mould him into a reliable breadwinner.[11]

This interpretation fits better with their own evolving social attitudes. The BSA data indicate that single mothers' views have changed a lot over the last twenty years. Up to a point this is simply a correlate of the fact that young mothers generally have been moving from a pro-career to a pro-domestic set of values. As predominantly young mothers, the category of lone mothers will have changed their values more than others. But the extent of their shift does seem to go beyond that of other, equally young mothers. In 1989 single mothers diverged noticeably from other mothers in a pro-work/female independence direction. But by 2006 their priorities had become very different.

This is supported by other data. If for example we apply the primary identity test, to divide mothers between those seeing themselves first of all as mothers and those choosing to think of themselves firstly as *women*, then single mothers turn out as rather more likely now to adopt a maternal, domestic identity. The mothers of younger children are generally more likely than those of older to select the private identity; so the following table (2.19) contains a gradation of children's ages to allow for this. It shows that as we move to *younger* mothers and children, single mothers are increasingly likely to be *more* domestic in their orientation than other mothers at the same parenting stage. So the difference is not just a function of age.

There is a variety of other evidence leading to the same conclusion. We have already seen that in 2006 single mothers were not obviously hostile to marriage as such. In addition to this, they were very close to other mothers on many moral and parenting issues. For example, single mothers agreed in detail with other mothers on the need to make divorce harder where there are children under the age of 16. On some questions single mothers proved a shade *more* conservative. Thus 69% of those with dependent children took an authoritarian line on the need for public censorship against 64% of mothers with partners, and young single mothers were more disapproving of extra-marital sex than mothers with partners, though not of *pre-marital!* Again, this prompts the observation that any hesitation they may have in relation to marriage could be due to a greater idealisation and caution on their part, rather than disdain for the institution itself.

Table 2.19 Primary identities of single mothers
(2006; row %)

% selecting primary identity as	Mother	Woman	Bases
WORKING AGE MOTHERS			
Single mothers	58	20	293
Mothers with partner	46	22	594
MOTHERS OF DEPENDENT CHILDREN			
Single mothers	68	17	183
Mothers with partner	56	21	345
MOTHERS OF DEP.T CHILDREN UNDER 13			
Single mothers	70	14	147
Mothers with partner	56	21	283
MOTHERS OF DEP.T CHILDREN UNDER 4			
Single mothers	74	13	57
Mothers with partner	56	20	126

It could be argued that single mothers of young children are more likely than others to be driven into domesticity because of the greater obstacles that they confront at work through not having a partner. This is not disputed here. But what must also be true is that over the last twenty years, as more mothers have gone out to work and experienced its difficulties for themselves, they would collectively have had many opportunities to try out different lifestyles and discuss the relative implications and merits of each. So the changes of behaviour and values over this period must to some extent mark the outcome of a process of selection, with the experience of being a single mother proving more compatible with certain circumstances than others.

Specifically, those mothers *keen* to work and follow careers will have been likely to find that having a male partner makes a valuable difference. For as we have seen, as more mothers have moved into work it is those with partners who have been able to increase both their rate of activity and the grade of their occupation most effectively. Single mothers by comparison have been rather left behind here, becoming relatively more domesticated and tied to childcare.

The corollary of this is that women not so keen on pursuing a career, but who do want to have children and are looking for a materially secure means of doing so, might well have found single motherhood a simple and convenient solution. Single mothers certainly do still contain many who are interested in working themselves, in order to support their children independently. But they may be a decreasing proportion of the total.

Several books have come out recently in the US which document the trend there for women who very much want to have children, but who for one reason or another do not have a male partner, to establish themselves as financially-independent mothers. These perhaps offer a different sort of example of women 'working for their families'. But this is not what appears to be happening in Britain, at least for the majority of single mothers. For in the UK there is another way. Mothers who do not wish to compete in the workplace can automatically claim state benefits which, while not generous by many people's standards, do at least deliver them from financial anxiety.[12] We saw just now (table 2.17) that in 2006 about half of single mothers in Britain with dependent children declared that state benefits provided their main income. This is a headache for policymakers. I suspect that it is also not such a boon for many single mothers themselves!

Being dependent on benefits is not much fun. Many commentators refer to the public stigma entailed. But equally or more important for many is the loss of autonomy. Traditional notions of marriage and motherhood gave most women a good deal of personal autonomy and control over their family lives. This was disputed and eventually undermined by campaigners like Eleanor Rathbone, who portrayed men as having an innate desire to subjugate women; their 'Turk Complex'.[13] She advocated a more interventionist approach by the state towards women to defeat this male tyranny. But the systems set up to provide direct supports to women may, in the event, now constitute at least as much challenge to a mother's authority, from social workers and benefit officers, as formerly received from male partners.

What makes women happy

Now, after many years of collective reiteration by voices for women that dependence on men is their main problem, with emphasis on paid work of their own as the best alternative, it seems that this may not be a majority view. It is noteworthy first of all that the status of living with 'no partner' is now the least happy economic condition for a woman to be in. This is *not* about widowhood. The next table (2.20) for all women of working age shows that in 2006 the 'neo-conventional' division of labour (that is, women working part-time with male partners working full-time) contained respondents who were much more content, both personally and in their family lives, than those living in financially independent households.

Secondly, and more broadly, it is instructive to note (in table 2.21) that those women who are most sympathetic to the welfare state and its collectivist solutions, which on the whole do not give much autonomy to citizens, tend to be rather less satisfied with their lives than women who *don't* put much faith in welfare. This is not just about being poor, as the 'sympathetic' category includes many who do not receive benefits themselves and believe in welfare altruistically as producing the best outcomes for a society as a whole. What may be at play here, once again, is the difference between women who attach primary importance to private lives and relationships and those who prioritise public roles. It is the latter who believe in welfare, and who are less happy in their lives. For the majority of women private life is central.

Table 2.20 Happiness by economic divisions of labour
(Row percentages)

(Women working age)

ECONOMIC DIVISION OF LABOUR	Satisfied with family life			Personally happy		
	Very	Fairly	Not	Very	Fairly	Not
Neo-conventional	78	19	3	59	35	7
Traditional	63	30	7	52	41	7
No partner	50	35	15	35	47	18

Bases: 119 Neo-conventional: 93 Traditional: 223 No partner   Source: BSA 2006

Table 2.21 Happiness by attachment to collectivism
(Row percentages)

(Women working age)

ATTITUDE TO WELFARE	Satisfied with family life			Personally happy		
	Very	Fairly	Not	Very	Fairly	Not
Sympathetic	56	35	9	45	38	17
Average	64	30	7	49	42	9
Hostile	66	31	3	76	19	4

Bases: 126 Sympathetic: 128 Average: 71 Hostile   Source: BSA 2006

This is, of course, not true of all women. Significantly – and although the numbers do get very small when we go to this level of analysis – it seems to be that the *happiest* single mothers are those who believe in the importance of work and are actually working themselves, often full-time. Interestingly, they also tend to be hostile towards state welfare, and may possibly be scornful too of those mothers who depend on it. They experience real autonomy as independent working women. The American model, perhaps! But there are not many single mothers in Britain who fit this pattern – perhaps approaching a quarter of the total at the moment.

Conversely, those single mothers who believe in family life, but are dependent on state benefits for financial support, form a group which is very far from content. There is not merely a manifest lack of personal autonomy in their lives, but also a glaring contradiction between what they most value and the road they have to follow in order to survive. Thus, just as the happiest category of all women are those who, working or otherwise, put family life at the centre and are themselves married, with attitudes and behaviour that are fully consistent, so too single mothers who believe in domesticity but are under constant pressure from the state to get a job are the *least* happy category. And I suspect that the current direction of social policy in Britain is not helping them at all.

The problem of men

This brings us back to the question this chapter started with – what is it that has happened to men, that so many women are choosing to manage without them? The short answer is that many men are drifting into marginality and un-productivity, where they are a burden on the community. In the traditional family system, a lot of pressure was put on boys to ensure that they became reliable workers who would then be marriageable family providers.[14] Over the past few decades the emphasis placed by a whole range of state institutions – including the education system - on female independence, plus the direct help given by welfare to women not able to support themselves or supported by men, has removed those constraints.

In passing, I should note that few see a direct link between male worklessness and increasing female participation in the workforce. The agreed underlying cause of male worklessness in Britain is de-industrialisation, perhaps aggravated by feminisation of subsequent new jobs.[15] But this may overlook some elements in the wider picture. British industry declined most catastrophically in the 1960s and 1970s, under competition from rebuilt European competitors and new producers arising in the East. This was at a time when girls were entering higher education at an accelerating rate, and the mainly-Labour governments of the period, firstly under the spiritual father of New Labour – Harold Wilson – took the strategic decision of investing in them and education, rather than trying to rebuild (or build new) industries to employ the men losing their jobs. It was the parting of the ways for the old working class and Labour: and the seeds of decay in working class family life were sown then. This may or may not have been the right strategy at the time for the economy. But we should not ignore the fact that it entailed a deliberate prioritisation of middle-class, female work, which signalled to working class men that they had become dispensable.

Whatever the precise nature of the relationship, though, as more women have entered the workforce, men have left it, giving us high (and growing) rates of male unemployment. And it is among those men who don't have partners expecting them to earn a family living that the worklessness is heaviest. Table 2.22 compares the economic activity rates of men in different age groups, in 2006, according to whether or not they were living with female partners.

Table 2.22   Men's economic activity by domestic arrangements

(All men; 2006 BSA)

	Man with female partner				Man without partner			
Age	18-34	35-49	50-64	65+	18-34	35-49	50-64	65+
ECONOMIC ACTIVITY								
Working	92	93	76	9	63	75	56	5
[Of which, *full* time]	90	89	69	3	50	73	52	2
Inactive	7	6	10	3	37	20	27	6
Retired	0	-	13	88	0	0	16	90
Looking after home	1	1	1	0	0	5	2	0
Bases	*194*	*390*	*273*	*244*	*245*	*179*	*171*	*183*

The differences are striking, and complement the figures on household divisions of labour given in tables at the beginning of this chapter. As shown in table 2.1, even men with partners are less likely to be working now than twenty years ago. But table 2.22 shows that men with partners are much *more* likely to be working than those without. This is arguably not simply a matter of women choosing partners who work – and indeed *expecting* men to do so. It is also that men who do not get the experience of living with and providing at least some support for a female partner may not develop the necessary motivations to hold down a job. There is a vicious circle operating. The private realm is important for men too, and their main source of motivation in the public. Playing it down in recent decades may have had all manner of unpalatable consequences.[16]

This data also shows how the traditional full-time housewife (and neo-conventional part-time housewife) may actually be much more productive economically within the community than they are usually given credit for. They are after all helping to organise and motivate a full-time working man, who would otherwise be state-dependent himself, or even drift into anti-social behaviour and criminality – another currently burgeoning area of male activity, which we have not considered here. Most ordinary women understand all this, and take it into consideration when making their life choices. It is just the political class and policymakers who don't want to know, and arguably sustain the system within which these problems multiply.

Conclusion and implications

The main sequence of findings examined here endorses the argument in the first chapter, which found that private realm concerns are in fact much more powerful among contemporary women than policymakers and their key advisors appear to understand. The fact that this applies equally to single mothers just underlines how important it is to recognise it.

Mothers managing without the support of a male partner tend in the main to be regarded either as simple victims of rough treatment by men, or as women who are so devoted to their careers that they do not want to be bothered carrying men as well as children. BSA surveys do not provide very direct data on attitudes to men and male work (and it is high time that they did). But there is plenty of indirect evidence, from women's own working patterns to their general social attitudes, to indicate that although the mould-breaking generation of single mothers may have had a real commitment to independent lives this is now far from normal. Single-motherhood is entered into earlier than it used to be, and increasingly before any effort at cohabitation has been made. There may often be a non-resident partner involved, so that in many cases single motherhood is just a first stage in a woman's career as a mother. Her interest in paid work is unlikely to be great. Indeed, if we combine single mothers describing themselves as unemployed with those 'looking after the home' it is clear that single-motherhood must have considerable appeal for a woman who just wants to be a housewife.[17]

From the data available on sources of income, the amount of single-motherhood in Britain does seem to be closely related both to the existence of relatively generous government supports – that is which enable a mother to set up an independent home for herself and her children at an earlier age than would be possible where she was creating a relationship with a male partner before having children – and also to low rates of employment among young men.

In terms of social policy, this all highlights the obvious question of why more emphasis is not placed on helping young women to settle with male partners sooner in their careers as mothers. This would have beneficial effects not only for children but also for fathers too, whose role in the community and economic motivations and commitment would all be strengthened. The current campaign by the Conservative Party to promote marriage is a big step in the right direction. But it may have only limited effect if it is not backed up by other measures. There is no doubt that marriage is the best state for couples and their children. But many single mothers already know this. The problem is that other state policies conflict with it. As long as policymakers give priority to getting *women* into work, push gender quotas for jobs that women don't actually want to do and are quick to provide independent homes for young single mothers, then they chip away at men's motivation to work and in the process reduce women's reasons to marry them.

There are of course numerous possible strategies for increasing male marriageability; too many to discuss here. But an education system which put more emphasis on giving *boys* skills they need to find employment, rather than leaving employers to rely so much on immigration to fill job vacancies; a tax regime which was fairer to poor couples – especially those with only one worker; greater awareness that broken families can be as damaging for children as material poverty; all of these point towards a variety of policy shifts which would assist more young women to find themselves husbands rather than becoming state dependents.

One final point. The growth of single motherhood also seems to reflect a desire on the part of most women to have children – even without a partner if that is necessary. Before second wave feminism, those women unable to find a husband in time were destined to become spinsters – who bestowed care on other women's children (as aunts, teachers and even nuns) if they had strong maternal drives. But the baby boomer feminists changed that, and encouraged women to feel that if they really wanted something then it was their right to have it. The data examined in this chapter does rather suggest, albeit indirectly as no BSA questions address the issue head on, that the desire of most women to become mothers is much stronger than their desire to be self-sufficient workers. An implication of this is that as medical advances continue to reduce problems of female infertility, we should anticipate that the 'right to be a mother' could quite easily replace rights to equal opportunities in the job market as the political priority of organised women's groups. It would be prudent for the state to have re-established the principle of individual male providers, as mothers' assumed source of economic support, *before* this happens.

CHAPTER 3   WIDER FAMILY TIES
– AND GRANDPARENTS

Networks of support

The help given by a male partner has to be looked at in the context of the wider network of support provided by the parents and adult relatives of a woman and those of her husband/partner. This multi-generational 'extended' family is in many respects the real family system at the heart of British society, and the heart of reciprocity in the moral economy. The smaller, co-residential 'nuclear' family, which we hear more about, is essentially just a concept convenient for – and encouraged by – the administration of public social services. This third chapter looks firstly at how this extended family system works in general in Britain, and then examines some problems which may be emerging within it at the moment and which could reduce its effectiveness.

Extended families in Britain

Britain is sometimes portrayed as different from its continental neighbours by virtue of having placed great emphasis on nuclear family life from very early times.[1] But this argument almost certainly attaches too much weight to the matter of co-residence. In Britain we can indeed go back a long way before finding much evidence of extended family *households*. But the work done by Peter Laslett and others makes it clear that separate households of small family units in historical times have always been accompanied by residence very *nearby* of some close kin – often in adjacent dwellings.[2] So domestic independence took place within the framework of larger active groupings of kin, which mediated an individual's membership of wider society. Differences with other cultures may not have been as sharp as sometimes claimed.

What is more, industrialisation – a process which is often seen as being linked with the supposedly minimal character of modern British family culture – may paradoxically have helped to *strengthen* those co-residential tendencies which British extended families did possess. Michael Anderson has shown how movement of young workers from villages in the nineteenth century into urban settings led to the development of three-generation households.[3] Most young mothers who worked outside of the home had a co-resident grandmother, who would look after the children in return for her own maintenance.[4] This sort of arrangement has probably been a factor promoting the overtly matriarchal aspect of British working class life, which distinguishes it both from rural British culture and also from the family patterns of most other countries.

But even if they were matriarchal, the idea of extended families conjured up unwelcome images of authoritarianism to postwar social revolutionaries in Britain. So as the welfare state blossomed it encouraged a hostility to grandparents (in particular) as being out of touch with modern realities, and too inclined to interfere in the lives of their offspring.[5] The nuclear family became the preferred model for social workers and other professionals. And insofar as people continued to live their lives within extended family networks, this was ignored and treated as something that was annoying but would eventually go away if ignored.

Rehabilitation of the extended family

There was however an ambivalence underlying this, not least because so many women in the pioneering baby boomer generation relied heavily on their own mother's help in looking after their children. As daughters, this cohort of women was quite keen to see the expansion of state services to take over care of their elderly mothers.[6] But as mothers they were often eager to arrange childcare within the family rather than using the public alternatives then available. Very many of them could not have pursued careers at all without the trustworthy and flexible domestic help of mothers who had not worked themselves or who, in the universal and effectively timeless manner of the babushka, gave up their own paid work when family duties called.[7]

This generation of women had started to become grandmothers themselves by the 1990s. Their ambivalent feelings then matured into a full-blooded recognition of the importance of this role, as the real centre of family life. Similar processes were taking place in other western societies where the private realm had also, albeit to a lesser extent, become displaced by the public. So grandparents – *les grands oubliés*, to adopt the poignant reference of Attiat-Donfut and Segalen [8] - were readmitted to the centre of our social life, where social policy has been trying to catch up with them ever since.

This was the background to the inclusion in BSA 1998 of a batch of questions on grandparenting.[9] Many organisations were interested to find out how useful contemporary grandparents were proving to be when it came to helping young mothers get back to work quickly. But in the event the survey findings which captured most public attention were those relating to grandparents as family guardians in a period when parental partnerships were becoming increasingly fragile. The survey revealed a considerable gulf between the lives of maternal and paternal grandparents. With the breakdown of parents' relationships, many paternal grandparents were becoming cut off from regular contact with their offspring. Meanwhile maternal grandparents were frequently finding themselves pulled into providing what were effectively crisis levels of support – which could be as stressful for them as having no contact at all.[10]

So this survey helped to draw attention to the role of grandparents in providing care for children and keeping family life on the rails and, in particular, enabling many single mothers to cope. For their part, single mothers showed great appreciation of this, and for example agreed strongly with the BSA survey proposition that working mothers needed the help of grandparents.[11]

Ten years have now passed since that study, and although there have been numerous other surveys carried out since which explore some of the topics in great detail it is not very clear how relevant its main conclusions remain. There are some issues which subsequent BSA data allow us to consider; but the nature of the data is different, and rather limited. That determines what is possible here.

BSA data available

We do not have any new BSA data which directly repeats the

questions used in the 1998 study concerning the content of relationships between grandparents and grandchildren. So for issues to do with grandparenting *behaviour,* we are still dependent on that survey. But there have been other questions exploring related areas.

Thus there have been three *Friends and Families* modules of questions contained within annual BSA surveys. These include questions relating to extended family life which, because they have been repeated a number of times, allow medium-term changes to be detected. The questions were run in 1986, 1995 and 2001, thereby bringing us closer to the present than our 1998 questions. Unfortunately most of these questions were only put to relatively small sub-samples of BSA; so case numbers are limited. However, so long as any analysis is kept quite simple this is not a problem, and the data *does* have some time depth - which helps in the identification of any major trends. So it does have definite value.

In addition to that, there are several questions in BSA surveys from 2001 onwards, inserted by the *Hera Trust,* which enable respondents with certain categories of relatives alive to be identified. Through these, we can pick out grandparents (including by whether they are maternal or paternal) and analyse their attitudes and characteristics. There are no questions on contact or kinship behaviour, so we cannot see whether grandparenting behaviour has changed since 1998. But *Grandparents Plus* has added more questions in the 2009 survey so that we will soon have more information on behaviour coming up.

What we have is therefore decidedly patchy. But the questions are important; and there is enough there for us to piece together sufficient information to address at least some of them.

The changing shape of families

Grandparents have been rehabilitated into extended families that are very different to those existing up to the middle of the last century. In the 1950s the structure of families was still quite short and fat – that is involving large numbers of adult siblings (and cousins) but rarely extending to more than three generations in depth. However, during the second half of that century fertility reduced considerably and longevity increased. So by the 1998 survey the generational pattern had changed to the more lineal, 'beanpole' structure which is now characteristic of modern industrial societies.[12] In this family pattern there are fewer same-generation relatives, but more generations in each family – arguably producing a more active role in family childcare for grandparents specifically.[13] These trends have continued since 1998. The first table here (3.1) shows that over the period of BSA surveys there has been a noticeable increase in the proportion of adult women whose own mother is alive.

Table 3.1 Women with mothers alive

% with mother still alive WOMEN OF WORKING AGE	1986	1994/5**	2001	2005-08
All	68	74	78	77
Childless women	84	85	91	88
Single mothers	67	75	77	74
Mothers with partners	62	68	72	71
Base range	*57-567*	*252-1182*	*71-366*	*1620-8131*
MOTHERS WITH DEP.T CHILD				
All	75	79	84	85
Single mothers	75	83	87	85
Mothers with partners	75	77	83	85
Base range	**-304*	*122-592*	*57-152*	*1052-2882*

Notes: Where base falls below 100, figure given in pale font. Asterisk denotes base under 50.

    **1994/5 Average for two years   (Mainly 95; one stream only in 1994)
    2005-08   Four years pooled and averaged
    1998 data not included here as not compatible

Within historical record there have been times when the presence of a maternal grandmother, even for very young children, seems to have been sufficiently uncertain and variable to constitute a real selective advantage. But we can see that in 1986 (the first year for which clear BSA data are available) 75% of the mothers of mothers with dependent children were alive. (This refers to children up to 17; so the rate for very young children is even higher.) By the period 2005-8 this had gone up further, to 85%; and the rate for all women under 60 had gone up from 68% to 77%. So clearly there are now rather few women bringing up children without the possibility of support from the maternal grandmother.

Meanwhile there seems to have been a continuing slight decline in the number of siblings. Table 3.2 gives the proportions of various categories of women under 60 who report having a sister alive.

Table 3.2 Women with sisters alive
(Column %)

(No question in 1994 or 1995)

% with sister alive	1986	1994/5	2001	2005-08
WOMEN OF WORKING AGE				
All	66		63	65
Childless women	54		64	59
Single mothers	84		64	70
Mothers with partners	67		62	66
Base range	*57-567*		*71-366*	*1620-8131*
MOTHERS WITH DEP.T CHILD				
All	73		66	68
Single mothers	82		70	71
Mothers with partners	71		65	67
Base range	**-304*		*57-152*	*1052-2882*

Note: 1994/5 - Question not asked. 2005-08 - Four years pooled and averaged

This shows that older women have more siblings than younger, so the lowest rates here are for childless women – who are on average younger. The figures in this table are least reliable for 2001, as they are based on a smallish sub-sample (compared to four full years, pooled and averaged, for 2005-8). But there probably is enough data to demonstrate the broad trend. At the same time as showing a general, slight decline in numbers, this table also gives some indication that single mothers are more likely than others to have sisters. This may give some further hints about the genesis of singlemotherhood; but at least part of the effect can be accounted for by class, in that single mothers are more likely to be working class, where fertility (and the size of sibling groups) is still higher.

Table 3.3 continues the picture.

Table 3.3 Women with grandchildren alive
(Column %)

	1998*	2001-04	2005-08
WOMEN ALL AGES			
Have grandchild	29	29	32
Have grandchild via son		19	21
Have grandchild via daughter		22	24
Base	*1810*	*8059*	*9608*
WOMEN WORKING AGE			
Have grandchild	15	15	14
Have grandchild via son		8	7
Have grandchild via daughter		11	10
Base	*1226*	*4342*	*6511*

Notes: % with GCs via son and GCs via daughter add up to more than all with GC, as many women have GC by *both* lines.
1998   No data for paternal/maternal GCs; questions only on selected grandchildren.
2001-04 & 2005-08 Four year periods, pooled and averaged.

Part of the 'beanpole' pattern is that more children have grandparents alive, and people are grandparents for more of their lives. Table 3.3 shows that even since 1998 there has been some increase in the proportion of women who are grandmothers. But this is not an indication of increasing fertility; it is simply a reflection of growing longevity. The figures in this table for *working age* women show in fact a reduction in the proportion of these younger women who are grandmothers in the most recent period.

This point is elaborated in table 3.4, which looks at the proportions of women who are grandmothers within 10-year age cohorts, for three selected years.

The proportion of women under 60 (and especially under 50) who are grandmothers is falling quite rapidly – following the rise in age at which women have their first child. At the same time the proportion of women above 60 who are grandmothers has *risen* – and especially for the over 70s. This again has not much to do with fertility and a lot to do with relative longevity. There has been some reduction in the proportion of older, childless women, as spinsters from the second world war have died off. But of greater moment here have been the medical advances which have disproportionately prolonged the lives of working class women – who contain higher proportions of grandmothers than middle class women.[14]

Table 3.4 Women with grandchildren – by age cohort
(Column %)

% of women with grandchildren by age	1998*	2003	2007
40-49	17	15	12
50-59	48	45	45
60-69	66	73	72
70-79	69	74	79
Base range	*199-291*	*258-424*	*256-421*

Contact with mothers

Simply having more grandmothers alive does not by itself mean that extended family relations are more important; just that they are possible for more people. In order to assess the relevance of these relationships, we need at least to look at rates of contact. Table 3.5 collates data from the 'friends and family' modules to see what can be deduced about changing levels of contact between women of working age and their own mothers, and how these link in with a woman's family status. This table contains two sets of figures, relating on one hand to simple frequency of contact and on the other to nearness of residence. The first two rows in the table (dealing with proportions of mothers dead, and where they are living in the same household) are common to *both* sets of figures.

Table 3.5 Women's contact with their mothers
(Column %)

(Women working age)

	1986			1995			2001		
	CLS	**SM**	**MwP**	**CLS**	**SM**	**MwP**	**CLS**	**SM**	**MwP**
No mother alive	16	31	37	15	23	27	9	23	28
Same household	44	8	1	28	12	2	24	3	0
See at least once a week	28	39	40	26	38	40	40	47	40
Tot. frequent contact**	72	47	41	54	50	42	64	50	40
See less than once a week	12	22	22	31	27	32	26	26	29
Base	*123*	*55*	*378*	*214*	*180*	*409*	*110*	*89*	*167*
Lives within 30 minutes	24	39	36	24	38	39	34	49	44
Lives further away	16	22	25	33	25	31	30	24	25

Notes: Two rows below *base* apply only if mother alive and *not* in HH
CLS = Childless; SM = Single mother; MWP = Mother with partner
**'Total frequent contact' row is simply sum of previous two rows, not an additional value for the variable

This table distils a lot of information, and needs quite a bit of commentary. To start with it adds detail to the point about growing longevity and falling numbers of women without a mother alive. This effect is masked in 2001 for women who are mothers (though not for the childless) by the fact that at the end of the century women were becoming mothers *later*. That is, mothers generally were getting older; so the proportion of them without mothers of their own alive did not change even though older women (especially grandmothers) were living longer.

Secondly, as more of their mothers have survived longer, fewer women co-reside with them.[15] The proportion of single mothers living with their own mother seems to have gone up in 1995 – endorsing the argument that many single mothers have been very dependent on parental support. The early 1990s were a period during which the number of single mothers was rising rapidly, and also when the importance of grandparents and the extended family was starting to be rediscovered. By 2001 co-residence had dropped a lot, perhaps reflecting the efficiency of New Labour in housing single parent families. But the frequency of contact by single mothers with their own mothers increased by the same amount, and if we add together the rows for living in the same household and having contact at least once a week (to give a *Total frequent contact* row) then the overall rate in 2001 stays the same.

For childless women, there is a noticeable reduction in contact with mothers in 1995, followed by a substantial rebound in 2001. The 1995 survey falls within the period when women were agreeing most vigorously with pro-work values. So it seems quite likely that the notion of extended family life held little appeal at this time, especially for young women who were just embarking on careers. It is noteworthy that the lower contact rate of childless women with mothers in 1995 coincided with a sharp increase (16% up to 33%) of them living more than half an hour's travelling time from their mothers. Francis McGlone and others concluded from their analysis of this data that in 1995 the contact rate of working women with their mothers had fallen to the same level as that for working men, reflecting the pre-occupation of both with work rather than family matters.[16] Looking now at the figures following for 2001, the early

1990s increasingly take on the appearance of a temporary blip.

It was very different anyway for mothers. As we have already seen, single mothers kept a steady (slightly rising) level of contact with their own mothers. They also recorded in 2001 a strong increase in the proportion living within half an hour's travelling time. Altogether they have done much to demonstrate the continuing relevance of extended family life in modern Britain. Mothers with partners have also maintained a steady contact rate with their own mothers throughout, and – notwithstanding an increase just in 1995 of the proportion living further away from them – have followed overall a gradual, longer-term trend of living *nearer* to them. So it seems likely that all mothers (single and partnered) have actively participated within extended family life at all times in the last few decades, regardless of the modernisation of women's lives. Childless women may have fluctuated more, according to where family life has figured in public realm evaluations.[17]

An examination of some extended family support activities can develop this point further.

Extended families in action

Families compared with other sources of help

The 'friends and families' sets of questions run periodically by BSA contain a number of questions examining people's views about where to seek certain types of personal support. The next three tables use data from them to show how different categories of women have responded to these over the period covered. These tables help to illustrate the part played by extended families at various stages of life, the different value placed on particular relatives in certain circumstances, and how these may have changed a little over time.

Support when ill

Firstly we look at help during short-term illness. The question put is: 'Suppose you had the flu and had to stay in bed for a while and needed help around the house, with shopping and so on. Who would you turn to first for help? And who would you turn to second?' Table 3.6 shows the sources of help chosen (from a pre-determined list) by single mothers, mothers with partners, and childless women, with first and second choices *combined* (with the result that these are not distinguishable here, and column percentages add up to more than 100%).

Although there is a good deal of common ground shared by these different categories of respondent, there are also significant variations. For single mothers, friends and neighbours emerge as the major overall source of support; though this is mainly on the basis of very strong 'second choice' listings. Surprisingly, perhaps, and by quite a margin, it is *children* who are single mothers' mainstay *first* choice in 1986 and 2001 (though shaded into second place by parents in 1995). But their second choice rankings are very low, and hence their overall standing is limited.

Table 3.6 Preferred sources of help when sick
(Column %)

(Women working age)   (Leading overall choice in bold type)

	SM			MWP			CLS		
	1986	1995	2001	1986	1995	2001	1986	1995	2001
Spouse/partner	16	19	23	**84**	**90**	**93**	59	52	52
Parent	25	**51**	41	20	28	33	**86**	**69**	**85**
Child	45	43	57	48	42	41			
Sibling	30	22	20	11	8	3	15	15	18
Other relative		9	11	6	11	8	9	6	6
Friend/neighbour	58	**51**	45	28	18	23	32	37	38
Paid help/ professional		3		1	2				
Base	*57*	*177*	*79*	*381*	*406*	*162*	*120*	*214*	*105*

Siblings were important in 1986, but have faded since then. 'Partners' on the other hand have been growing in importance over time, achieving fourth place overall in 2001. This is consistent with the way that single parenthood seems to have been changing.

Mothers with partners, by comparison, show a very heavy reliance on their partners, with virtually all of this preference (e.g. 92% out of the 93% expressed in 2001) recorded for 'first choice' help. Given this, children and parents both come in almost entirely as second choices; while siblings hardly figure at all. Their desire for help from outside the family, from friends and neighbours, is much lower than in the case of single mothers.

For childless women, partners are again, and consistently, the most popular *first* selection. But parents are quite strong as both first *and* second choices, and so are easily the preferred helpers overall. For childless women without co-resident partners, friends do figure as a valued source, albeit mainly as a second choice. Siblings come a long way behind.

Help with money

The second item here concerns responses to the question: 'Suppose you needed to borrow a large sum of money. Who would you turn to first for help? And who would you turn to second?' The pattern here is even simpler, boiling down largely to a contest between parents and 'professional' sources – meaning in this context public sources of finance, principally banks and other lenders or government agencies/social service departments. For single mothers there has been quite a dramatic shift from reliance primarily on public sources in 1986 to parents.

But this shift is not confined to single mothers. For mothers with partners, it is partners who have consistently represented the main first choice. But overall this has come behind public sources, principally banks; and it is mothers with partners who are probably in the strongest position of these three categories to approach a bank for money. But even with this category of women, recourse to public sources of credit has gone down in the period in question, with parents increasingly brought in to fill the gap. As life has become financially tighter, the extended family has recovered its central position! (And the figures here only go up to 2001!)

Table 3.7 Preferred sources of financial help
(Column %)

(Women working age)   (Leading overall choice in bold type)

	SM			MWP			CLS		
	1986	1995	2001	1986	1995	2001	1986	1995	2001
Spouse/partner	8	14	15	44	42	44	32	21	25
Parent	39	**57**	60	33	39	42	**73**	**78**	**83**
Child	16	14	9	12	10	8			
Sibling	21	25	21	12	11	9	6	15	11
Other relative	4	15	7	15	19	15	11	13	12
Friend/neighbour	21	24	26	6	5	3	7	6	8
Paid help/ professional	59	43	34	**63**	**60**	**56**	63	52	51
Base	*57*	*177*	*79*	*381*	*406*	*162*	*120*	*214*	*105*

With childless women, who are predominantly younger, the importance of extended family was probably never really in doubt. t In all years in this table parents have represented the main source of finance, with public agencies in second place; and over the years this rule has intensified.

Help when feeling down

The third type of support considered here relates to providing a sympathetic ear. The question runs: 'Suppose you felt just a bit down or depressed, and you wanted to talk about it. Who would you turn to first for help. And who would you turn to second?' This is an area where being an outsider, and impartial, may often be useful; and it is accordingly the topic where friends and neighbours come into their own. For all categories of women, this source figures strongly in all years; but there are also small but significant variations.

For mothers with partners, the partner himself is the main first choice as *confident*. Apart from 1995, when family ties were at a low ebb generally, this partner has been the main overall source of support. For single mothers, friends and neighbours have been the mainstay throughout, and in the absence of a male partner a range of relatives (child, parent, sibling) have provided some supplementary help. Partners too have played some part though, and it is interesting that in 2001 they have eased themselves into second overall position of support. In addition to reflecting (again) the changing character of single mothers, and their less independent orientation, this perhaps suggests that a revival of extended families may go along with a revival in the valuing of male partners too!

Table 3.8 Preferred sources of help when feeling down
(Column %)

(Women working age)	(Leading overall choice in bold type)								
	SM			**MWP**			**CLS**		
	1986	1995	2001	1986	1995	2001	1986	1995	2001
Spouse/partner	18	11	29	**65**	57	**72**	45	42	44
Parent	28	33	27	20	22	27	43	43	51
Child	42	18	24	25	16	18			
Sibling	28	27	22	20	23	13	16	20	22
Other relative	2	4	5	4	6	6	3	4	2
Friend/neighbour	66	**87**	74	49	60	52	**80**	**76**	**70**
Paid help/ professional	12	14	12	12	10	10	9	9	7
Base	*57*	*177*	*79*	*381*	*406*	*162*	*120*	*214*	*105*

For childless women, a male partner is the main first choice as *confident*, but fades strongly in the second choices. Friends and neighbours come out top overall here, throughout the period covered. Parents are also still very important to women in this stage of life, and have moved into second overall place in 2001 (based principally on a powerful 'second choice' showing).

Help in different life stages

The great strength of the extended family is that it provides the basis for mutual supports between different age and sex categories in every stage of life. Parents are the main source of support not just throughout childhood but also during the difficult transition to adulthood. But after this the balance changes and it is no longer comfortable to receive much more help than is given in return. The foregoing tables show how (young) childless women are in the process of transferring their dependence for help away from parents and onto a male partner, who may be seen as becoming a new member of the family, and certainly with whom there is a more directly reciprocal and therefore *in*dependent relationship.

But the question which obviously arises here is what happens to single mothers, who don't have a male partner to bring into the loop in the same way? A first response to this is that clearly (and as argued in the previous chapter) many single mothers *do* have male partners 'living apart', who to a greater or lesser extent play a similar part to fully co-resident partners. But insofar as there is no partner at all, single mothers are more reliant on friends; and it is often noted that single mothers have close friendships with other single mothers, with whom ties of reciprocal support are created.

But what also comes out of these tables, more generally, is that single mothers tend to draw on a wider range of sources of help than mothers with partners. In addition to 'friends and neighbours', parents are used more than by mothers with partners – though not massively more as single mothers are usually keen to avoid over-dependence. So there is still a margin to be made up. And where a good deal of this additional help for single mothers appears to come from is their *children*. That is, the co-resident (and often quite young) offspring of a single mother seem to take on a good deal of the general support that a resident male partner would be expected to provide.

This presumably changes the nature of the mother-child relationship, making it more equal and reciprocal. Certainly it produces different feelings about the relationship. There is an interesting question in BSA 2006, where respondents are invited to agree (or not) with the proposition that: 'The relationship between a parent and their child is stronger than the relationship between any couple.' As shown in table 3.9, this rings a bell with single mothers, who respond to it very approvingly.

Table 3.9 Views on strength of parent-child relationship

(Women working age)

Family status	SM	MWP	CLS
The relationship between a parent and their child is stronger than the relationship between any couple.:			
Agree	70	41	37
Neither/don't know	23	37	44
Disagree	7	22	19
Base	*246*	*513*	*325*

The importance of childcare

One area where single mothers are frequently seen as being particularly reliant on their own parents is help with childcare. All categories of mothers feel happiest leaving young children with a family member; especially with a grandmother, who combines un-questionable dedication with proven capacity and experience.[18] And for a single mother, lacking a partner to share basic care with, such support can make a critical difference.[19]

This is borne out by BSA data. The BSA survey year which examined this most thoroughly was 1994; the two tables which follow here summarise the relevant findings. Mothers were asked both about the childcare system which they actually used, and also what they thought would be ideal for them. Non-working mothers were asked both questions, but were invited for the second question to indicate what they felt would be their ideal if they *were* working (or, more to the point perhaps, would overcome any reservations they might harbour about going out to work at all).

Table 3.10 presents the findings on childcare arrangements actually used.

Table 3.10 Childcare currently used: 1994
(Column %)**

(Mothers with dependent children)

Current status	Working		Not working	
% using arrangement:-	SMs	MWPs	SMs	MWPs
Self (only works in school hours)	6	1		
Works from home	6	14		
Childminder	6	14	3	0
Relative	55	34	6	13
Friend or neighbour	13	11	12	4
Husband/partner	10	40	0	17
Nursery (including workplace)	10	7	13	8
None of these	3	1	72	64
Bases	*52*	*207*	*59*	*112*

** First and second choices combined; so add up to over 100%

This table confirms that whereas working mothers with partners depend heavily on being able to share childcare with those partners, single mothers are considerably more likely to use other kin - principally their mothers. Interestingly, a number of working single mothers do also get help from partners; but none of the non-working single mothers. Indeed, relatively few of the *non*-working mothers recorded any help at all with childcare, probably because they needed it less, but also perhaps because that term is mainly used to denote care specifically aimed at enabling a woman to work.

Table 3.11 shows mothers 'ideal' childcare arrangements.

Table 3.11 'Ideal childcare if working': 1994
(Column %)**

(Mothers with dependent children)

Current status % wanting arrangement:-	Working		Not working	
	SMs	MWPs	SMs	MWPs
Self (only work in school hours)	49	43	54	62
Work from home	19	15	9	17
Childminder	13	11	15	6
Relative	45	41	51	35
Friend or neighbour	16	8	18	12
Husband/partner	16	33	9	30
Day nursery	13	19	25	16
Workplace nursery	13	15	3	7
Bases	*52*	*207*	*59*	*112*

** First and second choices combined; so add up to over 100%

The chief difference between the actual pattern of childcare and the 'ideal' pattern shown in table 3.11 is that the most popular ideal arrangement, among single and partnered mothers alike, is where they would only work during school hours (and effectively would not need any help). This suggests both that many mothers were not very happy working at all until their children had reached school age, and also preferred to spend time themselves with their children when they were not actually at school.

In the pattern of ideal arrangements, single mothers again record the greater interest in grandparental childcare, though not by such a large margin. If partners are removed from the table, however, there are no other substantial differences in preference between the two categories of mothers. So for single mothers it does look as though grandparents have basically expanded their role to fill the gap created by the absence of resident partners.[20]

Extended families and working mothers

So extended families in Britain still remain at the centre of people's lives, and have continued to be a source of stability and assured care, over the last few decades. Recently they have been given some credit for this by the political class.[21] But it is not at all clear at the moment that they will be able to sustain this through many further transformations in women's lifestyles. What has protected them for the last generation is that, as multi-generational groupings where the centre of gravity lies with older people, they can absorb and deal with quite a lot of change in the lives of younger people.

But if changes of values and behaviour prove longer-term, and work through eventually into the lives of the older generations too, then crucial inter-generational exchanges may be affected. David Willetts is right to be concerned about this.[22]

There are two primary areas of concern here, to do with working mothers and the rise of single motherhood, both of which were flagged in the report to the 1998 study. We do not have fully equivalent sets of data since then to see exactly how things may have developed. But we do now have enough data to start making some preliminary assessments of what is going on, and to help identify what needs to be kept under observation.

A new division of generational labour?

The first question relates to the consequences of women withdrawing from the private realm of family life to spend more time in paid work. Many of those women who have themselves been most keen to immerse themselves in careers have also been very concerned to keep the care of children within the family. In 1980, when women in the baby boomer cohort were starting to take on new levels of responsibility in the marketplace, the government survey carried out among working women found that 44% of fulltime childcare was being performed by grandmothers![23] But what happens when this generation of working women becomes grandmothers themselves; will they want to leave their jobs to become babushkas in turn? And if not, can extended families go on providing the level of support that working mothers require?

At this point we have to remember that being a babushka is intimately linked with high valuation of the private realm. Those women who do leave their work to take on family care activities do not like to see themselves as carrying out a chore, but as assuming a senior and honoured role within the extended family. They welcome the position, as one of influence and authority. But already in 1998 there were indications that the role no longer carried the same status. Many grandmothers did not feel that they had much (or indeed any) say in how grandchildren were brought up; and even more mothers admitted that they did not allow any say to grandmothers.[24] Since baby boomers' reworking of motherhood, it was now mothers who decided how things should be done, and called the shots – leading to many grandmothers feeling either excluded, if they were not given any role, or put upon where they were told that they were needed but not allowed any authority or voice.[25]

By the time baby boomers had started to become grandmothers themselves, being a babushka was probably a much less desirable role than it had once been – and certainly not a position that a woman with a career would cheerfully put herself into. So in 1998 there were already signs that young grandmothers were less ready to take on the traditional role, and that boomers were continuing to innovate. We noted in our analysis of 1998 data that there seemed to be some movement towards a new generational division of labour. The grandmothers under 60 of young children under 13 (that is, those most implicated in childcare) showed a pattern whereby those who felt being a grandmother most rewarding, and felt closest to their grandchildren, were those who were working (especially part-time). They saw their grandchildren regularly, but they were not responsible for frequent childcare duties.

Those grandmothers who were the *most* happy with their lot were those working while the mothers of their grandchildren were *not*, and who were contributing money to the parents rather than providing intensive childcare for them.[26] An arrangement which was quite common, and seemed optimal in terms of both mothers' and grandmothers' levels of satisfaction, was where both were working part-time and childcare was divided between them.

There were in fact quite a large number of different patterns identifiable, though unfortunately none containing enough cases for very reliable analysis, nor one, single, dominant model evident. However, what *was* quite clear was that where mothers were working full-time the level of satisfaction of grandmothers was much lower.[27] We concluded that this:-

> "... may be a pointer to a new type of division of labour within an extended family, in which grandparents are closely involved with their grandchildren but much of the daily care is left to mothers themselves. As we have seen, the working but non-caring granny is able, and likely, to give money to her offspring. So it may be that as the effects of new career-patterns among women work their way through the family life-cycle, the support given by grandparents may increasingly take *either* financial or practical forms. Work and care are to some extent interchangeable, as they are for parents."[28]

Differing interpretations of evidence

A number of studies carried out since the 1998 survey have picked up, as we did, a sense that many contemporary grandparents are feeling burdened by the demands now being made on them by their children.[29] This has been interpreted by some commentators as evidence that grandmothers are being called on increasingly to provide care.[30] But I think that it is rather more likely, as we noted ourselves in the original report, that what is being picked up is the anxiety and even resentment of older women who have spent much of their lives in paid work and who do not relish giving it up to look after grandchildren. As noted earlier, many of this generation left much of the care of their own children to their own mothers, so that they could invest time in their careers. Now they had become grandmothers themselves, it made more sense to go on working and to make a financial contribution to the family rather than start taking on unfamiliar caring activities.

As we put it then:-

> "... what is arguably new therefore is not so much the pressure on grannies to do childcare as their *resistance* to it. The revolutionary generation of women who challenged and adapted convention as they passed through earlier life-stages are perhaps in revolt against the traditional expectation of daughters – which they exercised themselves as daughters – for family childcare support."[31]

Impact of the working granny

This latter interpretation does seem to fit the subsequent BSA data. We have seen earlier on (table 3.7) that mothers are turning to parents more often for financial help; and this is consistent with greater emphasis by grandmothers on working themselves. (It can also be seen as yet another way in which women's choice to do paid work is often motivated very directly by family considerations. Women who continue with careers can, after all, contribute more money to the family than the market value of those *caring* services which they do not provide. So at that level it is a justifiable substitution.) If we look also at available data on the economic participation of different age categories of women, this also points to changes in family working patterns.

Table 3.12 Changing economic participation of categories of women
(4-Y pooled figures)

% working of:-	1983-86	1987-91	1993-96	1997-00	2001-04	2005-08
Working age women	54	59	59	64	67	67
Women age 50-59	51	55	54	61	66	67
Mothers with dep.t children	43	50	51	58	63	62
Mothers with child under 13	35	44	48	54	60	58
Bases: WWA	*3281*	*4570*	*5270*	*4280*	*4342*	*6511*
50-59	*608*	*836*	*1014*	*905*	*1142*	*1359*
MWDCh	*1569*	*2132*	*2355*	*1904*	*2377*	*2597*
MWDCh<13	*1155*	*1643*	*1894*	*1435*	*1867*	*2048*

Table 3.12 shows how some categories of women have increased their economic participation more rapidly, at certain times, than other categories. Over the 25 years covered by this table, women as a whole have steadily increased their working rates (apart from just after the 1993 recession); reaching a peak by 2001-04. Young mothers have increased their rates most, starting with very rapid rises between 1983-86 and 1987-91, to achieve nearly average rates in 2001-04 – falling back slightly in 2005-08. Women aged 50-59 increased their participation at a fairly moderate pace up to 1997-00, but then have speeded up since and are the *only* category of women to actually go on increasing their participation since 2001-04! So as young mothers have slowed down, older women (coinciding, it should be noted, with the baby boom generation) have speeded up.

But it is not *all* baby boom women who do this. There is a strong 'family' orientation involved too. If we divide up the category of women aged 50-59 according to their family position, or generation, then the results are quite remarkable. We don't have the data to do this for all periods; but fortunately we do for the crucial periods 2001-04 and 2005-08, which is when it seems to get interesting. Table 3.13 shows the results.

Table 3.13 Recent changes in work rates among women 50-59
(4-Y pooled figures)

(Women age 50-59)

% women working, by family generation	2001-2004	2005-2008
Childless	68	62
Mothers but not grandmothers	73	72
Grandmothers	57	64
Bases: CLS	*202*	*230*
Mothers	*489*	*533*
Grandmothers	*594*	*658*

What this division tells us is that family motivation is the key here. Women without children do not, on the whole, have strong family incentives driving them to work; and it is in this category accordingly that we find most of the women who have taken early retirement. The percentage of them working drops considerably between the two periods considered as the proportion of them retiring early has gone up – possibly as the appeal of a career in itself fades for all age groups of women?

Mothers in this age group without grandchildren too are likely to have children who are predominantly self-sufficient. Thus although they have little to impede them from working, they don't have strong motivations for increasing their working rate either. So they stay just at about the same level; perhaps a shade down.

This brings us to grandmothers. Traditionally these are less likely to be working in their fifties than other women, as they have important family duties pulling them into retirement. That, presumably, is why they have the lowest working proportion of the three categories in 2001-04. However, grandmothers show a strong rise in that proportion in 2005-08. What is more, they are the *only* category here to show any increase in this period. In fact they are probably the only (sizeable) category of women of any age who do so; at the same time as mothers of young children are recording a decrease!

The implication is hard to resist. Over the last few years, grandmothers have been doing less childcare and mothers of young children have been doing more of it themselves and working *less*. It is not possible to say how much this is a matter of grannies being less available, or how much it is because younger women are deciding that they want to stay more at home anyway. On the basis of the data analysed here it seems likely to be a bit of each. This means that there are probably a number of different ways in which future balances of care and support within the extended family may be maintained.

Avoiding a deficit in family care for children

Extended families in Britain seem to be holding together well as networks for mutual care and support between generations. Within families, probably universally, older generations see their help in looking after children as a sort of indirect repayment for the care they received themselves when young. As well as this, older people also (historically in Britain and to this day still in many countries) help to look after children in anticipation of the further care and financial support they will need in old age. But this more direct form of reciprocity seems less strongly rooted in people's feelings.[32] So care for the elderly has been incorporated much more easily into the welfare systems of modern societies than the care of very young children.[33] Few mothers seem very happy to allow the state to become too prominent in controlling care of their children; and providing a reliable support system for carers is probably still the central process in extended families.[34]

This reliability could be threatened if the baby boomers' innovations were to lead to a deficit of family care. It has to be said, though, that there are no signs of this happening. For if the money now provided by working grannies helps young mothers who wish to stay at home, then the new division of labour still results in an overall exchange and balance.

However, the particular system now emerging may not have the same chances of survival as the conventional one it is replacing – whereby women only took paid work when there was no compelling family business calling them. The daughters of baby boomers now doing the bulk of their own childcare are less interested than their mothers were in pursuing successful careers which they will want to continue when they become grandmothers themselves. So for this new generation there could be a return to more traditional choices at each stage in their life-cycles – restoring a traditional pattern of family caring.

The question then becomes whether the baby boomers' strategy just represents a short-term blip, or whether it paves the way for a more complex set of options in the future. Various scenarios offer themselves, from a simple return to tradition, to a system where succeeding generations of women in a family tend to alternate between working and caring modes; or even one where women have children younger so that those interested in having a career don't embark on it seriously until after their children have reached a certain age. All of these models are feasible and compatible with extended family support systems, and lend themselves to homeostatic mechanisms whereby balances of work and caring are achieved in those families.

So changing work patterns in themselves do not herald an end to effective extended family life. However, when combined with the consequences of single motherhood such changes may give some real cause for concern. Table 3.14 looks in a bit more detail at what has been happening to working grannies in recent years. It takes all working age grannies (rather than just those 50 or over) and divides them between those who live with partners and the growing number who don't.

What this division shows is that there are two rather different trajectories being followed. The growth of work among grannies overall is driven by those with partners. They are both working more, and doing so more fulltime. Single grandmothers on the other hand (even if they don't still have dependent children of their own – as many of the younger ones do) are not just working a little less overall, but are doing so much *less* fulltime. Insofar as these single grandmothers may have single mother *daughters*, there is a very different type of extended family emerging here which needs our attention and consideration.

Table 3.14 Recent changes in work rates among grandmothers
(4-Y pooled figures)

(Grandmothers of working age)

% grandmothers working, by partner status	2001-2004		2005-2008	
Single grandmothers**	53		52	
(Of whom, working full-time)		41		33
(Of whom, working part-time)		12		19
Grandmothers with partners	60		65	
(Of whom, working full-time)		31		36
(Of whom, working part-time)		29		29
All grandmothers	58		62	
(Of whom, working full-time)		33		35
(Of whom, working part-time)		25		27
Bases: Single GMs		*266*		*310*
GMs with partner		*554*		*581*
All grandmothers		*834*		*898*

** Excluding widows, counted here as *with* partners. See definitions at beginning of chapter 2

Extended families without men

Two types of extended family

We noticed when analysing our 1998 data that lone motherhood had produced new patterns of grandparenting, according to lineage. The breakdown of parenting relationships typically increased the role of maternal grandparents, while often leaving the paternal effectively excluded. These effects are summarised here in table 3.15 – adapted from the original report.[35]

Table 3.15 Single parenting and the emergence of lineage differences
(1998 Column %)

(All grandparents with grandchildren under age of 13)

% of GPs who:-	Parents' relation	Maternal GP		Paternal GP	
		MGM	MGF	PGM	PGF
Have had no contact	Together	0	4	0	3
with GC in last 2 years	Apart	4	11	10	35
See GC several times a	Together	30	31	34	34
week or more often	Apart	54	32	14	12
Speak on phone with	Together	27	18	24	12
GC several times a week or more	Apart	35	18	10	6
Visit friends or	Together	14	11	16	11
relatives with GC at least once a month	Apart	43	14	10	0
Exchange presents	Together	46	42	43	38
with GC at least once a month	Apart	61	37	20	12
Bases	*Together*	*174*	*115*	*147*	*93*
	Apart	*	*	*	*

* (Base under 50)

The 'apart' bases in this table are small: but the pattern of associations is so strong that it shines through all the random variations. Where parents are together, both sets of grandparents are equally involved with the grandchildren and the only systematic difference is due to sex – that is between grandmothers and grandfathers. But where parents are apart, lineage comes into play as the dominant factor. When combined with the effects of sex – themselves strong – lineage produces a gradient of involvement in which maternal grandmothers are the most heavily involved and paternal grandfathers the least.

Since 1998 the number of lone mothers has continued to rise, and has also affected grandmothers more too. Table 3.16 documents some of the key trends.

Table 3.16 Development of matrilineal extended families
a. Proportions of lone mothers/grandmothers
(Column %)

(Women all ages)

% of:-	1998	2001-04	2005-08
Mothers who <u>alone</u> (but not grandmothers)	18	23	24
Grandmothers who <u>alone</u> *	9	14	15
Grandmothers who are <u>under 55</u>	25	23	17
Grandmothers under age 55 who are <u>alone</u>	15	25	27
Single GMs under 55 who are <u>Maternal</u>	61	69	74
Bases:- *Mothers (who not GM)*	815	3383	3999
Grandmothers	574	2625	3282
Grandmothers under 55	116	494	528
Lone grandmothers under 55	*	185	243

What is particularly interesting here is that as the proportion of young grandmothers (under 55) has fallen, the proportion of these who are *lone* grandmothers has increased. That is, and presumably related to the trend to younger, never-partnered lone *mothers*, there appears to be a divergence taking place between grandmothers with partners – who are getting older – and lone grandmothers who are not, and may even be getting younger. And an increasing proportion of these younger, lone grandmothers are maternal, suggesting that many of them could also be the mothers of today's young lone *mothers*. Three-generation extended families without men appear to have arrived.

This is confirmed by all of the pertinent direct measures which BSA does contain. For the year 1998 (in our grandparenting module) and since 2006 there are questions in the survey concerning whether or not the parents of respondents' grandchildren are together. This enables us to compare the extent to which lone mothers may be producing daughters who become lone mothers themselves.[36] To this end, table 3.17 collates the findings for maternal grandmothers, who would be the key figures in any emerging three-generation female-centred extended families.

Table 3.17 Development of matrilineal extended families
b. Three-generational lone motherhood
(Column %)

(Working age MGMs with grandchild under 16)

	1998		2006-08	
% MGMs with:-	MGM is SM	MGM is WP	MGM is SM	MGM is WP
Daughter who SM	44	28	53	42
Daughter who MWP	56	71	47	58
Base	*	79	183	337

Again, sample numbers for lone grandmothers in 1998 are small, so that year may not be a reliable baseline for assessing trends. Nevertheless, insofar as it is, these figures do suggest that there may be a growing tendency for these lone mothers ('MGM is SM') to have daughters who are lone mothers themselves (up from 44% in 1998 to 53% - of a larger proportion of women - in 2006-08).[37] However, even if there has *not* actually been any increase in the self-reproduction rate of lone mothers since 1998, the future multiplication of female-centred extended families seems assured. If more than half (53%) of the daughters of lone grandmothers are now lone mothers themselves, plus approaching half (42%) of the daughters of grandmothers who do have partners, then to put it bluntly we now seem to be in a phase of consolidation and growth.

Drift towards underclass

The problem with this new type of extended family is that it seems liable to become very inward-looking, and in the last analysis be parasitic on the rest of society with more conventional families. This is because the primary focus of such families seems bound to lie around issues of personal care of their own. In this they are taking support and services from other sectors of society without contributing very much in return. As a family system it is not self-sustaining: it needs to have other types of extended family in society to provide for it. In fact this system would appear to lead inexorably towards Charles Murray's nightmare of an unproductive and socially dependent underclass.

The heart of the matter is that single mothers do not seem very interested in working. They are more interested in the ultimately more rewarding and important (though always needing support) business of mothering – that is having children and caring for them. Traditionally they would not have been able to do this without finding male partners and motivating them to help as family providers. But the welfare state has changed all that, by stepping in as a direct provider itself – rendering many potentially helpful men redundant in the process.[38] So it should be no surprise that a new type of extended family is appearing which is organised around caring, and consumption, rather than a mixture and *balance* of production and caring.

This can be illustrated by looking at the economic dimension of this type of extended family. Table 3.18 compares data relating to maternal grandmothers for 1998, 2001-04 and 2005-08.

Table 3.18 The economic role of MGMs

(Maternal grandmothers)

% MGMs who:-	All MGM 1998		MGM working age					
			1998		2001-04		2005-08	
	MGM is SM	MGM has P	MGM is SM	MGM has P	MGM is SM	MGM has P	MGM is SM	MGM has P
WORK STATUS								
Working	36	31	47[+]	70[+]	50	58	51	65
Inactive	21	5	32	8	37	9	35	13
Retired	29	47	5	2	1	8	1	6
Looking after home	14	17	16	20	12	25	13	16
MAIN INCOME SOURCE								
Job & family	36	39	47	81	52	73	51	75
Savings/pr. pension	7	20		5	3	10	3	11
State pension	25	34		4	1	4		2
Benefits	32	7	53	9	43	12	46	11
DAUGHTER** WORKING?								
Full-time	17	26	17	23				
Part-time	21	39	22	39				
Not	63	35	61	38				
RECENTLY GIVEN MONEY TO GC PARENTS								
Have helped out	43	40	56	53				
Have not	57	60	44	47				
Base	50	276	*	84	185	401	243	461

* (base below 50)   [+]See chapter note 42   ** i.e. mother of grandchild

For 1998, figures are included here both for '*all* women' and for 'women of working age'. It is the latter category which is relevant for comparison with the later periods; but again, the base numbers of lone grandmothers in that year are very small. So the figures for all women are given here too, as the pattern they show is very much the same (apart from the presence and knock-on effect of retired women) while the base totals, although still rather small for the lone grandmother category, are large enough to lend some weight to the findings.

What the main pattern here indicates is that lone MGMs are rather like younger lone mothers in their economic behaviour, with relatively low rates of working and high rates of inactivity.[40] But the most striking data in this table surely derives from the question in 1998 (and not repeated since) on their daughters' economic participation.[41] For a daughter of a *lone* MGM seems to have a much lower probability of working than the daughter of an MGM with a partner.[42] This suggests that, even back then, a culture of domesticity could have been developing in extended families headed by lone MGMs.

We can explore this phenomenon a bit further, from the perspective of the middle generation. Table 3.19 collates data for a number of years where we can tell whether or not a respondent's mother is alive. This will help us to see if there is any obvious connection between having a mother alive (so possibly available for childcare duties) and a woman actually having a job.

These findings are quite revealing. For mothers with partners, that is those who are part of an extended family system which is fully plugged into wider society and productive activities, having a mother alive has in recent years – from the mid-nineties at any rate - been clearly linked with a *higher* level of economic participation. These grandmothers probably did play a very important role in getting young mothers working during the period of their increasing participation. But for a mother without a male partner, having a mother alive is linked more often than not with a *lower* level of participation. This suggests that many mothers of lone mothers (whether actually lone or not themselves) may be heading extended families that are committed to caring rather than productive activities.

Table 3.19 Mothers' economic participation – by whether own mother alive

(Mothers with dependent children)

% working of:- SINGLE MOTHERS	1986	1995	2001/2003**	2005-08
Mother alive	27	29	55	49
Mother not alive	30	42	42	56
MOTHERS WITH PARTNERS				
Mother alive	48	61	68	67
Mother not alive	57	59	52	63
Bases: SM MA	*	66	192	889
SM NM	*	*	*	155
MWP MA	184	237	542	1550
MWP NM	62	54	105	203

* Base under 50

** Mainly 2003. One stream of 2001. None of 2002

However this does not seem to apply to single mothers for the period 2001/3; and this could indicate one of two things. Firstly it could simply be that base numbers for lone mothers without mothers alive are so often small that (except for 2005-08) the periodic variations shown are in fact mainly random. Or alternatively it could mean that the first few years of this century *were* actually different from other periods. We know that this is when the working levels of young mothers reached a peak, and it may be that in these circumstances (with pressure on mothers to work, perhaps, and a prevailing public culture prioritising work) more mothers of young lone mothers *did* provide a type of support more conducive to working than has been the case before or since.

We cannot resolve this from the data available, and so cannot establish what trend may be running here. But we do at least know with confidence that for the period 2005-2008 at any rate, during which there has also been clear evidence for the existence of a different type of extended family among many lone mothers, there *has* been a different pattern of maternal influence on single and partnered mothers' work activity. The data for this period is moreover extensive enough (when pooled) to allow quite detailed analysis. The final batch of tables in this chapter draw on this to examine the work behaviour and the main income source of mothers, according not only to whether their own mothers are alive or not but also to the age of children. This will help to clarify and summarise differences between conventional and female-centred extended families.

Table 3.20 looks at the proportions of various categories of mothers who are working.

Table 3.20 Economic activity by mother alive and youngest child's age
(Column %: 2005-2008 pooled data)

% working of:-	Mothers working age	Mothers w/ dep.t child	Mothers w/ ch. under 13	Mothers w/ ch. under 4
SINGLE MOTHERS				
Mother alive	53	49	44	29
Mother not alive	58	56	48	27
MOTHERS WITH PARTNERS				
Mother alive	69	67	64	55
Mother not alive	65	63	56	40
Bases: SM MA	*1200*	*889*	*702*	*271*
SM NM	*401*	*155*	*106*	***
MWP MA	*2130*	*1550*	*1284*	*610*
MWP NM	*831*	*203*	*173*	*53*

* Base under 50

Table 3.21 deals with the proportions of mothers who are not working but looking after the home.

Table 3.21 Economic activity by mother alive and youngest child's age
(Column %: 2005-2008 pooled data)

% looking after home of:-	Mothers working age	Mothers w/ dep.t child	Mothers w/ ch. under 13	Mothers w/ ch. under 4
SINGLE MOTHERS				
Mother alive	25	29	34	51
Mother not alive	16	23	30	63
MOTHERS WITH PARTNERS				
Mother alive	24	28	31	41
Mother not alive	18	27	37	57
Bases: SM MA	*1200*	*889*	*702*	*271*
SM NM	*401*	*155*	*106*	***
MWP MA	*2130*	*1550*	*1284*	*610*
MWP NM	*831*	*203*	*173*	*53*

* Base under 50

As we have seen already in previous chapters, mothers are less likely to be working, and more likely to be looking after the home, if they have young children; and lone mothers are overall less likely to be working. The figures in tables 3.20 and 3.21 reflect all this rather neatly. They also show how having a mother alive affects lone and partnered mothers in opposite ways, pulling the former into domesticity and the latter into work. These differences are greater when children are younger – which is when the part played by a maternal grandmother could be the decisive factor influencing what a mother does.

Table 3.22 uses the same frame of variables to look at how mothers' households derive their main financial support. Here the pattern is not quite so strong, pointing to the action of other factors, especially where there are young children. The 'income from job/family' item includes a woman's own earnings, those of a spouse, *plus* any financial help given by parents. For mothers with partners, this category provides the great bulk of family income at all child ages. But for single mothers it is only when children are older (and there is no mother alive) that family earnings begin to figure as the main income source.

Table 3.22   Main source of income by mother alive and youngest child's age   (Column %: 2005-2008 pooled data)

% main HH income from job/family:-	Mothers working age	Mothers w/ dep.t child	Mothers w/ ch. under 13	Mothers w/ ch. under 4
SINGLE MOTHERS				
Mother alive	52	47	41	28
Mother not alive	59	52	45	27
MOTHERS WITH PARTNERS				
Mother alive	91	93	93	91
Mother not alive	81	91	93	95
% main HH income from benefits:-				
SINGLE MOTHERS				
Mother alive	46	52	58	71
Mother not alive	38	46	53	67
MOTHERS WITH PARTNERS				
Mother alive	6	6	7	9
Mother not alive	7	7	7	5
Bases: SM MA	*1200*	*889*	*702*	*271*
SM NM	*401*	*155*	*106*	***
MWP MA	*2130*	*1550*	*1284*	*610*
MWP NM	*831*	*203*	*173*	*53*

* Base under 50

The other important source of family income for mothers is state benefits. This is hardly resorted to at all by mothers with partners. But for single mothers, in particular for those with mothers alive, this appears to represent an indispensable prop. It is not possible to discover just from this data exactly why having a mother alive increases a lone mother's dependence on benefits. It could be that this trend in the figures reflects the shift to extended families without men. When a single mother has *conventional* parents, she is likely to be kept by them within mainstream society, where she may find not only a partner more easily but also work when she wants it. Where she is part of an extended family without men, all of this seems much less likely. But it may simply be that if lone mothers do in fact value domestic life as much as the previous chapter suggests, then having a mother alive to share it all with (especially the parenting of children) may render available benefits even more attractive than where there is no maternal grandmother.

Conclusion and implications

The findings analysed in this chapter underline even further the importance of tackling male worklessness in Britain, and bringing men back into useful, productive roles in families and the community. Extended families constitute essential networks of personal interdependence, which maximise support for mothers raising children. They continue to do this. But the rise of lone motherhood, now extending into senior family generations, poses a threat to their effective operation.

This may be easy to discount or overlook, because the proximate dangers to children themselves are commonly not great. Extended families articulated around single mothers give very great attention to the needs of children, and can indeed be models of solicitude. The problem is that they may do little else, and *that* is what weakens the wider community which these families form part of. In themselves, extended families without men fit well into ruling social conventions and policies and can be seen as a reasonable adaptation by women to present social realities. Children can suffer if they are excluded from contact with fathers and paternal relatives. But the main costs of the new system are borne by fathers, the many mothers who miss the companionship of a husband, paternal grandmothers, and the wider community when considered as a functioning entity.

The conventional extended family operates as a very effective mechanism for maintaining a balanced and productive community. Women are often transformed by motherhood into fuller citizens, with greater understanding of others. But it is men who are normally changed most by family life and coming to experience the needs of other family members – mainly but not exclusively their own wives and children. This is often what makes them into caring and useful members of society. Men tied into extended families as partners, and best of all as husbands, are far more motivated to hold down jobs and perform other roles in the community, in order to increase family capital. Those on the other hand who are liberated from such responsibilities are not merely less useful, but are also much more likely to become a drain on society, by drifting into disorganised states and criminality.

It is the loss and waste of male resources which is the basic flaw in extended families without men. The women in these new families are not the sort who want to take over male roles. They neither do enough paid work or other production in the public realm themselves, *nor* provide sufficient incentives for free-floating men to make up the short-fall. So they generate a serious and growing deficit, which can only be balanced in wider society insofar as members of conventional families do more than their fair share. The caring carried out in extended families without men is paid for (via state benefits) by mothers with partners (who do more paid work than lone mothers) and their mothers (likewise) and not least by their male partners. New class conflicts are brewing here. This is not a pattern of redistribution which is popular in the wider community or viable in the long run.

CHAPTER 4   REPRESENTING WOMEN

Sisters of the revolution

The three preceding chapters should have made it clear that there is a great deal of support among women in Britain for their traditional place at the centre of the private realm of family and 'informal' relationships. And this support definitely appears to be growing. But one would never guess this just by listening to current policymakers. Virtually nothing is said by major parties about the importance of families in local community life. The airwaves are heavy instead with commitments to strengthening equal opportunities and bringing more women into work. This can be anticipated from the *Women and Work Commission.* But when the leader of the Conservative Party prepares for an election by promising a land of Work and Opportunity, and the senior woman in the party attacks those who stay at home by declaring that it is disgraceful that more are not out at work, it is clear that British society is broken.

So how is this happening? How are politicians failing to pick up on what women want? The answer revolves I think around the issue of differential access to the public ear. And the main *problem* here seems to be that the increased direct involvement of women in the public realm has undermined the traditional mechanisms whereby the needs and interests of the private realm used to be represented and made influential.

In the traditional society which so many commentators are quick to declare themselves glad to see the back of, the specific interests of women were identified explicitly with the private realm, and indeed seen as its core. These interests were brought into the public realm, and policy, by being communicated *within* the private realm to men such as husbands, sons, brothers and any others in a woman's circle who might be in a position to help promote them. The public realm was predominantly male, and so men were the channels to it.

The drawbacks of this system have been given a lot of attention; but it did also have two great benefits, which have not yet been adequately substituted. Firstly, and in quite a diffuse way, it meant that all men were made very aware – certainly more so than today – of what the women in their lives actually wanted. It got men's commitment to the private realm and made them conscious of its importance. It civilised them. Secondly, and more directly to the point here, it meant that those people charged with actually representing women's interests in the public domain had little chance to redefine or interfere with them. Men only enjoyed any legitimacy on such topics by virtue of their role as voices on behalf of women. This was understood all round, and meant that men would be subject to constant scrutiny – and rebuke if they muddled the message.

This system was soon dispensed with once growing numbers of women started to have careers themselves in the public realm, and moved into positions where they could influence public attitudes and policies directly. But a likely drawback of this *new* arrangement is that while giving a direct voice to those women who have moved into prominent positions it may easily result in neglect of the views of others. Women given a direct voice have a *personal* legitimacy which male spokesmen never enjoyed; so there is less incentive for them to listen to others – particularly to women who do not share their views. So the representation of women's views may well have become narrower than when it was filtered through men. Those women now speaking *for* women may even consciously feel sometimes that they should *not* listen too hard to others anyway, as these are bound to include many who do not understand what is going on. Revolutionaries know best.

Boomers at the helm

This is also to some extent a generation thing. Those women with public voices were for a long time younger than average, and could easily see any who might disagree with them as being out of touch and past it. The revolution in attitudes which has informed the thrust for equality in the public realm was pioneered by the young women moving through higher education into careers during the

1960s and 1970s. It was experienced – as indeed many revolutions are – as being one of youth and hope for the future against the restrictions and cynicism and compromises imposed by age and authority – including in this case patriarchy. Sisterhood ruled. The desire for public equality was grounded in private frustrations. And an assumption made by women active in the movement, which still holds to this day, has been that sisters will carry on supporting it until its objectives are fully achieved.[1]

But sisters may not include daughters. For in the event this revolution does seem to have been especially identified with one generation or cohort, with younger women proving less enthusiastic. In a recent paper elsewhere, I have characterised these active women, born from the mid 1940s until late 1950s, as belonging to the generation of 'choice'.[2] They can be seen as united historically by the fact that traditional family life was still strong during their childhood and even into young adulthood; but at the same time welfare state supports were also opening up, boosting their opportunities as free individuals. And they grew up in a booming economy.[3] So they enjoyed maximum choice, embracing both the private and public realms. This group corresponds to the original 'baby boomer' generation.

What separates this cohort from those coming after, and may account for the failure of younger women to believe so passionately in its goals, is its enthusiasm for the welfare state. For the choice generation, the welfare state was an unambiguous good, opening doors to new lives for women; not least as professionals within its own proliferating services as functions previously carried out in the private realm became relocated to the public. Younger generations of women have been more exposed to negative aspects of this process, as the growth of welfare became accompanied by a weakening of conventional family life and the local communities built on this. So they are more circumspect. As the following table illustrates, in 2006 (when the choice generation were aged 50-64) overall sympathy among women for the welfare state was highest among the choice generation and those coming immediately after it.

Table 4.1 Support for welfare system by age/generation
(Column %)

(All women)

Age/generation	18-34	35-49	50-64 'Choice'	65+
ATTITUDE TO WELFARE				
Sympathetic	29	37	38	30
Average	43	39	43	46
Hostile	29	23	18	24
Bases	*386*	*444*	*401*	*327*

Source: BSA 2006

This cohort effect is detectable throughout the measures which have figured in this analysis. But because of the effect of motherhood it is not always immediately apparent. Becoming a mother introduces a woman to experiences and feelings which pull her into greater awareness of the private realm. So to see the cohort effect we need to separate mothers from women without children. The next table shows what happens when this is done. However, when analysis is taken to this level the numbers in some categories start to get too small to be reliable. So in the following table men are left in too. The pattern is the same (though not so marked); but the figures are a bit more reliable. The next table (4.2) is therefore, strictly speaking, about parenthood rather than motherhood.

What it shows is that parents' attitudes are more in tune with traditional domesticity than are those of non-parents. But this is not uniform across all generations. This shows up in two main ways. The *gap* in attitudes between the responses of the oldest (and most traditional) respondents and the choice generation is considerably larger among the childless than among parents. For example, the gap between the oldest and choice generations for agreement with the proposition that being a housewife is fulfilling stands at 21 percentage points (56 down to 35) for childless respondents, and just 12 (54 to 42) among parents. Also, the *spread* of responses between generations is greater among the childless. Thus among parents the range in support for the idea that family life suffers if women work full-time is only 8 percentage points (i.e. 43% among the oldest generation, down to 35% in the youngest). But this goes up to 37 points for childless respondents (59% for the oldest, down to 22% for the youngest). That is, attitudes are more similar among parents of different ages than they are for childless respondents. Parents of all ages seem to be largely united by their common life experiences. Childless respondents on the other hand appear to remain more influenced, and so divided, by age-specific public ideologies dominant at formative stages in their lives. And the group which stand out as *most* different in all of this is the choice generation – separated by quite a gulf from the traditional respondents preceding them, and then increasingly left behind by successive *younger* generations as these move back to more traditional positions.

Table 4.2 Family values by age/generation and whether parent
(Column %)

(All women and men)

Age/generation	18-34	35-49	50-64 'Choice'	65+
% agree that:-				
Being housewife as fulfilling as paid work				
Parent	49	42	42	54
Childless	37	36	35	56
Family life suffers when woman has full-time job				
Parent	35	35	36	43
Childless	22	38	35	59
Watching children grow is life's greatest joy				
Parent	55	30	34	37
Childless	18	21	18	35
Base range	*182-441*	*124-710*	*76-629*	*59-633*

Note: Where base falls below 100, figure given in pale font. Asterisk denotes base under 50.   Source: BSA 2006

In terms of the current representation of women's views, it is obviously very significant that the choice generation of baby-boomers contains most of the women who are now at the peak of their careers and influence. Their ability to get their own opinions converted into public policy is almost inevitably greater than their simple numbers would warrant.

The class basis of sisterhood

What started out largely as a revolt of the young against age and authority may have transmuted since into a class issue. For the choice generation contains the first group of women in Britain to penetrate deeply into professional life. Their pro-work values are very consistent with the demands of professional lifestyle and culture, and within this environment there has been much stronger adoption and retention of the new value system by later generations. Pro-work attitudes pioneered by the choice generation have for some time now been particularly well established among professional workers. And insofar as these views have disproportionate influence on public policy, this may be helping to generate new sorts of divisions between women.

Class and values

During the 1960s and 1970s young women in Britain were entering careers as never before. And this new-found enthusiasm for paid work has remained a significant feature of our middle class sub-culture through to the present day. The next few tables chart some aspects of this.[4] [Please note that for most of the measures included in tables 4.3 to 4.5, response levels given do **not** indicate the percentages of respondents who are **agreeing** with propositions. Instead they give the percentages who **don't disagree**.

The reason for this is that on these measures there are large numbers of neutral and undecided responses, which reduce both the 'agree' and 'disagree' figures. So presenting *only* those who agree with a view has the effect of making it appear to be more of a minority viewpoint than it actually is. For our purposes up to this point that has not mattered. But when discussing class, it is important to be able to demonstrate not only how middle class opinions consistently differ from other peoples', but *also* that on a number of important issues the middle class view is the minority position. All of the 'agree-disagree' propositions included in these tables are pro domestic life rather than pro work; and it is by *dis*agreeing with several of these that the middle class respondents are expressing a minority view. However, it would be rather confusing for the argument to have to reverse the content of the tables to show the proportions who *disagree*. Instead the neutral responses have been added to 'agree', to produce 'not disagree' figures. Please bear in mind that this is not the same thing as agree.]

Table 4.3 Women's ideas about work and children, by class
(Key years)

(% of All women)   (No questions in 1986 & 1998)

	1986	1990	1994	1998	2002	2006
% not disagree that a pre-school child is likely to suffer if his or her mother works						
Middle class		57	46		41	43
Intermediate		67	53		56	54
Working class		65	57		54	53
% agree that a mother of a pre-school child should stay at home						
Middle class		44	37		33	32
Intermediate		62	51		50	38
Working class		60	59		52	40
Base ranges: *Middle*		*243-303*	*106-285*		*267-323*	*229-298*
Inter		*395-508*	*140-229*		*232-312*	*203-283*
Working		*320-437*	*123-435*		*271-431*	*250-374*

The two measures in table 4.3 approach the issue of the effect of a working mother on children from different angles, but come up with very similar results. Both confirm that middle class women have been distinctly less inclined than others to consider mothers' work a risk to children. Both also show that other women have been catching up with middle class opinion-leadership here, and have in fact adopted pro-work views rather more rapidly than these have grown among middle class women themselves. So there has been a marked convergence since 1990, in a pro-work direction (which has probably been assisted by the expansion of part-time working). But on the direct question of children suffering, middle class women are (still, and just) the only group where those who at the moment 'do not disagree' with the proposition are a minority.

It is noteworthy that here, and elsewhere, the views of 'Intermediate' and 'Working' class women show little difference. This merits a brief comment, (and I have discussed this in more detail elsewhere)[5]. The main point to note is that on family matters there is not a simple gradient to be found between Middle and Working class respondents, as Intermediate workers do not form a transitional group between, or constitute an overlap of, the two other groups. On quite a number of issues, it is the Intermediate rather than Working class who themselves emerge as the more clearly pro-family and anti-work. Several reasons can be put forward for this. But one that is particularly relevant here I think is that the Intermediate class of women contains quite a number of wives and partners of middle class men. That is, were they to be classified in terms of their family attributes and lifestyle rather than their own jobs they would be counted as middle class. And the reason why many of them are not middle class in their own right, through their own occupations, is that these are middle class women who are choosing **not** to prioritise work. They have not pursued careers because they do not believe that this is good for their families. So they take other jobs which are less demanding. In this way the Intermediate category provides a refuge for otherwise 'middle-class' women who reject the dominant female culture in that class; and this pulls the responses of this category in a pro-domestic direction. It also helps underline for us the minority character of many aspects of middle class female culture.

Table 4.4 Women's ideas about work and family life, by class
(Key years)

(% of All women)

% not disagreeing that:-	1986*	1990	1994	1998	2002	2006
A man's job is to earn money and a woman's job is to look after the home and family						
Middle class	37	26	21	33	18	27
Intermediate	57	39	38	39	32	36
Working class	71	49	52	39	42	41
Family life suffers when the woman has a full-time job						
Middle class		53	48	48	45	47
Intermediate		63	50	56	57	58
Working class		64	50	48	59	57
Base ranges: Middle	158	304-05	285-86	242	322	298
Inter	290	507-08	329-31	196	311-12	283-87
Working	287	434-39	334-36	347	431-34	372-74

*In fact 1984, as question not asked in 1986.

The first measure in table 4.4 is the proposition on sex roles which has come to enjoy almost talismanic status in mainstream accounts of women's changing position. The figures here confirm that middle class women in the mid 1980s were considerably more hostile than others to assumptions entailing a division of labour. Since then approval levels have dropped steadily in all classes (with smallish samples in the mid 1990s probably contributing to some minor fluctuations). Again, lower class opinion has followed the middle class lead, producing some convergence. But unlike in table 4.3, there are signs here that there has lately been some movement the other way as well, as young middle class women rediscover domestic pleasures. But the overall class gradient, although less steep, still remains. With the second measure, there is very little evidence of change over the period covered, once neutral responses have been added to agreement. But there is a modest class difference there, which is persistent. The middle class women are the only ones among whom there is not a clear majority, most of the time, for not disagreeing that full-time work has harmful consequences for family life. When it comes to evaluating domestic roles directly, in table 4.5, there is even clearer indication that middle class women are essentially in a minority position.

Table 4.5 Women's feelings about domestic role, by class
(Key years)

(% of All women) (Question not asked in 1998)

% not disagree that:- A job is all right, but most women want home and children	1986*	1990**	1994	1998	2002	2006
Middle class	38	40	33		35	44
Intermediate	46	50	44		46	57
Working class	61	64	59		56	67
Being housewife is as fulfilling as paid work						
Middle class		52	64		64	71
Intermediate		69	66		65	73
Working class		65	69		73	80
Bases: Middle	135	152-305	286		321-22	299
Inter	248	244-506	231		310-12	282
Working	243	269-537	432-35		430-33	375

*In fact 1984, as question not asked in 1986. **Ditto 1989; for measure 2.

When indecisive responses are added to agreement, both of these measures indicate at least a general reduction of hostility towards domestic life over the period in question, and even a strengthening of pro-domestic sentiment. And the lead here appears to be in working class hands. For the first attitude, it is *only* middle class women who consistently have a majority disagreeing that most women want a home and children. When it comes to idea that being a housewife can be fulfilling, there is a similar class differential here as on other measures. However, disagreement with this proposition has declined markedly since 1990, and this has taken place even more rapidly among middle than working class respondents. In this area middle class opinion has retreated to a point where pro-paid work responses not just a minority, but a *small* minority.

Overall, therefore, it is clear that there are established class differences in values here, with middle class women the chief advocates of paid work. But the differential is reducing, partly through a continuing (but decelerating) spread of pro-work values to women in lower classes but also through some (mainly recent) softening of middle class attitudes towards the private realm.

Class and motherhood

A further measure of the middle class pre-occupation with work is given by figures showing the proportions of women in each class who are mothers. Motherhood is closely related both to values *and* actual economic behaviour. Table 4.6 presents the changing incidence (by class) of motherhood in key years since 1986. There are quite a few small fluctuations over this period, relating to short-term circumstances. But longer-term trends reflecting fundamental values and their consequences are pretty clear, certainly for the middle and working classes – though less so for the more complicated 'intermediate' group.

What these figures demonstrate is that the pro-work values held by middle class women are related to much lower rates of motherhood. It has to been remembered here that 'childless' does not mean that a woman never has children, but has not done so at the time of the study. So a good deal of the middle class effect may simply be a matter of delayed motherhood. Women with a career are likely to leave having children until later. Some of them never will have children; but most will do so, after an extended childless period.

Table 4.6 Class and motherhood
(Key years)

(% of Working age women)

	1986	1990	1994	1998	2002	2006
MIDDLE CLASS						
Mothers	70	68	62	64	63	62
Childless	30	32	38	36	37	38
INTERMEDIATE CLASS						
Mothers	76	67	71	72	68	73
Childless	24	33	29	29	33	27
WORKING CLASS						
Mothers	89	83	78	83	76	74
Childless	11	17	22	17	24	26
Bases: *Middle*	*115*	*276*	*362*	*375*	*429*	*502*
Intermediate	*232*	*444*	*488*	*405*	*363*	*449*
Working	*206*	*361*	*418*	*403*	*477*	*616*

The continuing attachment of middle class women to these values has seen a continuing rise in the childlessness rate; though since the mid 1990s it has levelled off. Just as lower class women have been adopting pro-work *values* over the last couple of decades, so too their rate of childlessness has been climbing too, though it remains behind that of those in middle class occupations.

We will now look at how these pro-work attitudes, and their convergence, are reflected in actual working behaviour.

Class and differential rates of working

Their greater enthusiasm for paid work meant that middle class women soon achieved higher rates of formal economic participation than the working class, who had had to work whether they wanted to or not. As table 4.7 details, this differential was well established by the mid 1980s when BSA surveys began, and has carried on since.

Table 4.7   Class and economic activity from 1986
(Key years)

(% of Working age women)

	1986	1990	1994	1998	2002	2006
MIDDLE CLASS						
Working	71	75	75	80	81	82
Inactive	7	10	8	9	8	6
Looking after home	21	14	14	10	9	10
INTERMEDIATE CLASS						
Working	63	64	63	72	81	75
Inactive	6	6	11	11	8	10
Looking after home	30	29	26	16	10	13
WORKING CLASS						
Working	56	49	52	59	54	56
Inactive	11	12	19	16	22	21
Looking after home	33	38	28	25	22	22
Bases: Middle	*238*	*276*	*357*	*373*	*428*	*502*
Intermediate	*469*	*443*	*480*	*404*	*360*	*439*
Working	*434*	*361*	*408*	*404*	*474*	*611*

What is made clear by table 4.7 is the extent to which the growth in women's labour force participation in the last couple of decades has actually been concentrated in the upper part of the market. Women in professional and managerial jobs have not only increased as a proportion of all women, but have stepped up their work-rate too, at the expense of the housewife category. Women in intermediate occupations have declined as an overall proportion of all women, but have offset this by increasing their work-rate very steeply – though with a significant step back recently. A feature of this group is the way that the proportion of them living as housewives fell sharply during the Blair years, a decade after the equivalent fall among middle class women.

Only working class women have gone against the trend of increasing paid work. In spite of their taking on middle class attitudes, and delaying childbirth, their economic participation remains at the same level now as twenty years earlier, with a few ups and downs in between. The proportion of women in this category recording themselves as housewives has fallen a good deal, following the pattern among higher status women. But this has not led to higher levels of economic participation, only of 'inactivity'. What this adds up to is that they have become increasingly dependent on benefits, rather than being supported by a male provider. It is likely that this working class pattern has been heavily influenced non-working young single mothers.

A further picture of the class distribution of paid work is given if we look at the division of respondents between full-time and part-time jobs (in table 4.8).

Class differences express themselves in a slightly different way here. A substantial majority of professional workers have been, and still are, full-time. There was a small movement over to part-time working for professional and intermediate workers in the aftermath of the 1993 recession, which became long-term in the case of the latter group. But as a general rule, middle class women have remained strongly committed to full-time work and intermediate have favoured it. Basically women with careers and responsible jobs prefer to work full-time, except for short periods when they have very young children. Only among working class women is there a definite majority of part-time workers.

Table 4.8 Full-time and part-time working by class
(Key years)

(% of Working age women)	1986	1990	1994	1998	2002	2006
MIDDLE CLASS						
Working full-time	57	60	54	61	63	61
Working part-time	15	15	21	18	18	21
INTERMEDIATE CLASS						
Working full-time	43	42	36	36	52	46
Working part-time	20	22	26	36	28	28
WORKING CLASS						
Working full-time	26	21	24	25	24	28
Working part-time	31	28	27	34	30	27
Bases: *Middle*	*238*	*275*	*357*	*370*	*426*	*501*
Intermediate	*464*	*441*	*478*	*404*	*360*	*439*
Working	*432*	*361*	*408*	*405*	*474*	*615*

So it is women with less demanding and rewarding jobs who seem to have the best chance to combine paid work with significant amounts of time spent as mothers active in the private realm. And this raises some important questions about how women with different lifestyles manage to achieve their respective satisfaction and happiness. These are not easy issues to examine here as the data is limited. But even though our answers are necessarily tentative there is just enough material to allow us to address some central questions.

Class, work and contentment

The BSA questions relating to levels of contentment are only administered to quite small samples. This makes it impossible to do any complex analysis involving several factors at the same time. Instead we have to look at things from different angles, with limited combinations of variables at a time. We start here by simply looking at the relation between women's economic status and contentment, without considering class differences at all or even making allowance for motherhood. Doing this gives us just about enough cases for analysis.

Table 4.9   Contentment and economic status
(Column %)

(Women working age. 2006)

	Working		Not working	
	Full-time	Part-time	'Inactive'	Housewife
SATISFIED WITH FAMILY LIFE				
Very	63	72	54	56
Fairly	33	25	28	37
Not	5	4	18	7
PERSONALLY HAPPY				
Very	54	56	33	41
Fairly	37	38	44	46
Not	9	6	23	14
Base	*289*	*178*	*103*	*112*

Source: BSA 2006

Table 4.9 confirms that women working part-time are definitely more satisfied with their family lives than those working full-time, and also perhaps slightly happier personally. (Women 'not working' are generally less happy, though this does not apply to mothers[6]).

This still leaves the key issue of class somewhat in the air; and in order to deal with this at all we now have to compromise. To start with, we certainly have to go on leaving out the factor of motherhood. And even then we have to tolerate a number of quite small column bases. In that spirit we can look at two further tables, each of which gives a partial (but complementary) analysis of the class factor, from different angles. Firstly table 4.10 concentrates on *working* women, and looks at the way that class relates to their differential contentment according to whether they work part-time or full-time. Then table 4.11 re-combines full and part-time workers, and also unemployed women and housewives, in order to do a class comparison of working versus *non*-working women.

Table 4.10 Contentment by time spent working, and class

(Women Working Age. 2006)

Class	Middle		Intermediate		Working	
Time working	FT	PT	FT	PT	FT	PT
SATISFIED WITH FAMILY LIFE						
Very	66	75	62	66	57	76
Fairly	28	21	35	31	39	22
Not	6	4	2	4	4	2
PERSONALLY HAPPY						
Very	60	57	51	52	43	58
Fairly	33	34	38	41	43	39
Not	6	9	11	7	14	3
Bases:	141	*	88	64	60	66

Note: Where base falls below 100, figure given in pale font. Asterisk denotes base under 50.

There does seem to be a very clear pattern running through these findings, which could help clarify the relationship between women's work and contentment. Looking firstly at satisfaction with family life, it is evident that in all class groups it is the women working part-time who are the happier. The levels of contentment of full-time workers are however dependent on class, with the proportion of 'very satisfied' decreasing as one moves *down* each class step.

For personal happiness, the class differences are even more pervasive. The happiest middle class women are, by a small margin, those working full-time, presumably because more of the happiness of career women comes from work itself rather than family life. For working class women the opposite seems to apply. As their happiness derives much more from family life, full-time working is related to a good deal of unhappiness for them. Intermediate women are for once where we might expect them to be; in between.

The patterns in this half of the table are extremely neat – which given the small numbers of cases may indicate a very powerful effect. Even at the 'not happy' end of the table there is a strong tendency visible here, with *more* full-time working women reporting themselves unhappy as you step down by class (6, 11, 14) while part-time working women become *less* unhappy (9, 7 and 3). This sums up class responses to working very succinctly!

But neat and compelling as they are, these class differences in contentment which relate to *modes* of working are not as great as those associated with *not* working at all. Table 4.11 regroups the data so that we can contrast the class patterns on this. What the figures show overall is that it is overwhelmingly lower class women who are economically inactive – including for longer maternity breaks than in higher echelons.[7] And it is here that the sharpest and most dramatic class differences seem to lie. Most interestingly, it is these lower class *non*-working women who display the highest levels of discontent.

This sort of finding is frequently misunderstood. Pro-work commentators looking at these figures would have little hesitation in declaring that they simply exemplify the importance of ensuring that more women are enabled to enter the labour market. But this disregards the fact that lower class women who are inactive tend to have strongly pro-*domestic* orientations. They are not unhappy because they can't get or keep appropriate work. It is much more likely that they are unhappy because they would like to be leading active lives in the private realm of family and community affairs, but are instead required to register for work, and sometimes take jobs, in order to get the state benefits they need to care for their children.

Table 4.11 Contentment by whether working, and class

(Women Working Age. 2006)

Class Economic state	Middle class		Intermediate		Working class	
	Work	Not work	Work	Not work	Work	Not work
SATISFIED WITH FAMILY LIFE						
Very	68	60	63	55	67	51
Fairly	26	37	33	38	30	30
Not	6	3	4	7	3	19
PERSONALLY HAPPY						
Very	60	46	51	46	51	36
Fairly	34	47	39	35	41	43
Not	7	7	9	19	8	21
Bases:	*189*	*	*152*	*	*126*	*116*

What the data here keeps bringing us back to is that a high proportion of these unhappy lower class women are unemployed single mothers. Many don't want to work. Their discontent is rooted in their lack of personal relationships rather than in the world of work.

Pursuing this analysis into the private realm reduces our available cases even further; so any conclusions drawn from the following table may be far from robust. But for illustrative purposes, even if not for convincing analysis, it is useful to examine exactly where the cases of discontent seem to cluster most heavily. Table 4.12 compares the contentment rates for categories of single mothers with those of mothers with partners.

Table 4.12 Single motherhood and levels of contentment

(Women Working Age. 2006)

Variable	Single mothers			Mothers with partners		
Economic category	Work ing	In- active	Hous ewife	Work ing	In- active	Hous ewife
SATISFIED WITH FAMILY LIFE						
Very	59	32	46	69	62	62
Fairly	32	44	41	29	27	34
Not	9	24	14	3	12	4
PERSONALLY HAPPY						
Very	42	20	23	59	46	49
Fairly	50	36	50	34	39	43
Not	6	44	27	8	15	8
Bases:	85	*	*	228	*	70

The outcome is very striking. Those single mothers who are working are less contented than *all* categories of mothers with partners; but *more* contented than single mothers not working. They contain most of the older, pro-work (and pro-independence) type of single mothers; and the level of discontent they experience is presumably sustained in large part by the practical difficulties of their lifestyle. But those who are not working, and who report themselves as inactive or housewives, record *extremely* high levels of dissatisfaction with their family lives, and even *higher* rates of personal unhappiness. The younger that single mothers are, the more likely this seems to be their fate – though numbers are far too small by this stage in the analysis to show this reliably.

Even partnered mothers who describe themselves as economically inactive record quite high levels of discontent here. And again I would speculate that this comes down to living in a country which does not value domesticity and the private realm. Many of these women probably do not want to have to work. But there is little other source of public respect available to them; and they almost certainly need the money to be gained from signing on. So they are in a hard place.

Unequal public concern

The phenomenon of unhappy housewives is not given much attention at the moment by sociologists and policymakers. There is on the other hand a great deal of very sympathetic research devoted to the problems of middle class women who face obstacles to their careers. They are the ones we are urged to assist through new adjustments to social policy. Researchers like Rosemary Crompton and Clare Lyonette have demonstrated that career women who have unsupportive husbands – that is who do not pull their weight in household chores – are more likely to feel unhappy with their lives. They cannot find the time they need to cope properly with their jobs.[8] So Labour policymakers are thinking up ways to restrict the amount of paid work that all men do, in the hope of encouraging men generally to take on more domestic tasks.

There is no equivalent public sympathy for women who find that putting a lot of time and effort, unpaid, into running the private realm of family and community life does not elicit much recognition or reward.[9] But surely this traditional arena of female endeavour and social contribution is just where the greatest encouragement is currently needed in British society, and where the largest number of unhappy women are gathered. This is a result of the concentration of representative power in the hands of middle class women who are pre-occupied by their own concerns.

However, there may be a political solution brewing. For while the mainstream parties have been falling over each other to help middle class women promote their careers, there seems to have been a political alienation gathering pace among lower class women with different values. This is a situation which could eventually lead to a cultural counter-revolution.

The political challenge

By about twenty years ago the main public institutions of British society had been pretty well taken over by the notion of meritocracy, in which citizens have to earn their place in society through their paid work. It may not be a coincidence that since then political alienation has developed among ordinary people. This shows up in BSA surveys in the growing numbers of respondents who do not declare support for a particular political party. This is not the same thing as lack of interest in politics, the level of which has not changed greatly over this period.[10] These respondents just support 'no party'; and what this probably denotes is a lack of belief among them that any established party is going to pursue policies promoting things which they value.

The rise of 'no party'

Table 4.13 traces the development of support for 'no party' since 1986. There has been a near doubling of this response, overall, since 1986. It is noteworthy however that this has grown more among women than men, more among younger women than older, and significantly more among those categories of women (single mothers, housewives and so on) whom we have identified as least happy with their lot.

A *direct* link can also be shown between support for no party and not being happy, in that 16% of 'no party' supporters reported themselves not happy in 2006, as against 11% of supporters of *all* parties.[11]

For working age women as a whole, support for 'no party' doubled over this twenty years. For housewives it trebled, with an early jump in 1994 possibly suggesting a reaction against the IPPR pro-work campaign. While for single mothers, who were strong Labour supporters until the late 1990s, it nearly quadrupled – again with some early rise in 1994.

Table 4.13 Rising support for 'No Party', 1986-2006
(% of specified groups declaring support for no party)

	1986	1990	1994	1998	2002	2006
Working age women	9	10	9	13	15	18
Women age 18-34	11	12	11	16	19	22
(Working age) single mothers	7	7	13	18	23	25
(Working age) housewives	8	10	16	21	17	24
'Inactive' working age women	9	11	6	20	23	23
[ALL MEN]	8	8	8	12	14	15
Base range	*66-1249*	*124-1131*	*171-1315*	*172-1269*	*188-1388*	*228-1632*

Support for no party also shows some connection with self-identification as being *without* political influence. A question used by BSA to measure this sentiment invites respondents to agree (or not) with the proposition 'People like me don't have any say about what the government does'. Table 4.14 sets out the results for this, for those categories of women we have concentrated on.

Single mothers and 'inactive' workers (mainly unemployed) score well over average, while housewives are somewhat below average on agreement (with a large neutral response). This probably indicates that single mothers and the unemployed (who overlap a good deal anyway) have both developed some political self-consciousness, while housewives have not (yet) done so.

There is also quite strong overlap of this variable with 'no party' supporters, backing up the idea that many who do not identify with a particular party do have an awareness of being alienated to a certain extent.

Table 4.14 Experience of political alienation. 2006
(Column % of specified section of working age women)

Category of working age woman	All WWA	All 'No party'	Single mother	In-active	House wife	Age 18-34
People like me don't have any say about what the gov.t does						
Agree	47	58	64	67	40	49
Neutral/don't know	30	37	20	17	45	26
Disagree	23	5	16	16	15	25
Base range	*382*	*64*	*83*	*51*	*66*	*148*

Note: Most of columns have small bases, as alienation question put to one stream of respondents only.

But even if they are not already consciously mobilising, they may come to do so. For those values which give most explicit endorsement to the housewife role are positively associated with supporting no party. Table 4.15 takes four attitudes which value private realm activities and charts the proportions of supporters of four political parties (Conservatives, Labour, Lib-Dem and No Party) agreeing with them in 2006.

Two levels of agreement are used here, 'Agree' in a general sense, and 'Agree strongly'. Doing this shows that the stronger the level of agreement, the greater the difference recorded between 'No Party' supporters and other respondents. No other party supporters give such strong and consistent support to traditional private realm values as do 'No Party supporters.

The inference to be drawn from this is that discontent with major parties' policies in this area is likely to be an important factor prompting current political alienation among women.

Table 4.15 Agreement with pro-domestic values, by party supported

(All women and men)

Party supported	Conser-vative	Labour	Lib-Dem	No party
Being housewife as fulfilling as paid work				
All who agree	48	44	49	54
Agree *strongly*	10	6	8	14
Job is OK but woman wants home and child				
All who agree	21	32	13	32
Agree *strongly*	6	3	2	8
Man earns money; woman looks after home/ children				
All who agree	7	9	4	17
Agree *strongly*	0	1	0	4
Watching children grow is life's greatest joy				
All who agree	79	83	72	87
Agree *strongly*	26	36	23	39
Base range	*129-130*	*212-218*	*106-107*	*123-124*

Source: BSA 2006

Implications for main parties

In traditional, pre-meritocratic British society, many women favoured the Conservative Party, which was seen as the party of marriage and the family. This rule held quite well right up to the beginning of the BSA surveys; and among *older* women it still does

apply. But the rise of New Labour in the early 1990s disrupted the pattern. A strong bid was made by Labour for the female vote (for Worcester Woman) in order to break the Conservative hold. As a result there was a large transfer of women's votes into Labour through the 1990s. The two next tables, 4.16 and 4.17, document this by showing the change in party support declared by women in BSA surveys.

Table 4.16 Support declared by women for the Conservative Party

	1986	1990	1994	1998	2002	2006
All women	33	36	27	26	25	25
Working age women	30	33	24	22	21	21
(Working age) housewives	36	33	23	24	16	20
(Working age) mothers w/partnr	29	34	25	26	25	25
(Working age) single mothers	21	26	21	16	14	14
'Inactive' working age women	19	25	21	13	17	15
[ALL MEN]	30	33	24	22	21	21
Base range	*66-1249*	*124-1131*	*171-1315*	*172-1269*	*188-1388*	*228-1632*

These tables also show that by 2002 many women had become disillusioned with New Labour, and even more by 2006. However, not many seem to have returned (by then) to the Conservative fold. And the data examined here a little earlier indicates that this may be because the latter have adopted pro-work values and policies themselves. If this is the case then we can anticipate some volatility in the female vote for some time to come – perhaps until a major party makes a move to court traditionalist female opinion. At the moment the only party which does speak with approval about the private realm seems to be the BNP. This could be one of the sources of its growing success in old Labour heartlands.

Table 4.17 Support declared by women for the Labour Party

	1986	1990	1994	1998	2002	2006
All women	33	35	40	45	41	31
Working age women	35	36	40	48	42	30
(Working age) housewives	35	37	42	39	45	35
(Working age) mothers w/partnr	35	33	40	47	42	30
(Working age) single mothers	43	51	45	49	40	34
'Inactive' working age women	48	41	47	48	37	25
[ALL MEN]	37	43	41	44	41	35
Base range	*66-1249*	*124-1131*	*171-1315*	*172-1269*	*188-1388*	*228-1632*

New Labour and housewives

An aspect of this shift of women's political support which is particularly salient – as it takes us firmly back to the central issue of class – is the pattern of change among working class housewives. For among this category of women, mainly mothers, who are at the heart of local community life in most parts of Britain, there does not appear ever to have been a period of enthusiasm for New Labour. It is as if these women decided at the outset of Labour's drive to increase its female vote by appealing to working women that this would entail a corresponding loss of interest in mothers and traditional community life.

During the 1990s when Labour was becoming more popular among most categories of women, its support among working class women who described their occupation as looking after the home did not go up, but instead showed signs of weakening. It wavered a bit through the first Labour administration but then fell quite heavily by 2006 – along with other groups of women who had warmed to Labour earlier but were now disillusioned. If we add in figures for 2008 here, these show that between 2006 and 2008 the support for Labour among this group of women (who had once been very loyal to the party) collapsed seriously.

Strategists in all parties may well feel that this is not very important, as housewives and stay-at-home mothers are a dying breed. But that would be a mistake. All the evidence of the preceding chapters points to an ongoing revival of enthusiasm for this role, and of renewed recognition of its social importance. Labour dedication to opportunities for women in the workplace may well have alienated a section of the electorate which is actually starting to become more significant again.

Table 4.18   Shift of support out of Labour Party by working class housewives

(Working Age, Working Class Women 'Looking after the Home'

% supporting:-	1986	1990	1994	1998	2002	2006	2008
Labour Party	52	49	48	46	49	40	27
'No Party'	10	13	16	24	24	29	32
Base	145	135	118	105	117	149	132

Sisterhood and motherhood

So far in this analysis I have stayed very close to the data. But in this final section I am allowing myself the self-indulgence of a little theorising, to put it all in perspective.

The development of female classes

[Men's success in work] *bothers employment career women, who see men of average ability succeeding in places where women barely get through the door. It is entirely acceptable to women following the homemaker career, who are spending their spouse's earnings and profits. . Women's .... lack of* solidarity *vis a vis men is due to their having two avenues of upward mobility and achievement in life, through the marriage market or through the labour market.* (Catherine Hakim, 1996)

The movement of women's concerns out of the private realm was originally seen by many of its advocates as promising greater equality between them: sisterhood to replace what to younger women appeared as authoritarianism in family relationships. But this does not seem to have happened: the rise of careers has coincided with development of new forms of inequality between women, and arguably weakened them collectively in relation to men.

In the traditional society which is being left behind, senior generations of women (mothers and grandmothers) certainly exercised family authority over younger women (not to mention over most men). But this was a seniority which most could expect to achieve at some time in their lives, so it embodied a sort of equality too. It also entailed a good deal of female solidarity in the public realm. At the heart of the state's recognition of the importance of family life was an over-riding respect for motherhood: all mothers, whatever the class of their husbands, were to some extent drawn together by their common position and interests. (This is sometimes seen as a major source of popularity of the modern royal family, which is able to unite the nation precisely because it is a family like others.)[12]

In contrast to this, the sisterhood of shared equal rights in the public realm involves a lot of conflict and division. The data discussed in these pages can leave little doubt that different categories of women now have very divergent interests, so that no single set of social policies is going to please all of them. And some of them are more powerful than others. Policymakers have been failing for many years to listen to what ordinary women think. It is the viewpoint of middle class careerists - which has turned out all too often in this analysis to be a *minority* view - that has been dominant. For a while this might have been justifiable, on the grounds that opinions on these matters were changing fast, so that most women would soon catch up with policy. But it is no longer possible to believe this. A large (but not powerful) body of women have never abandoned pro-domestic orientations; and young women are now moving back to this position. The female careerist model seems likely to become increasingly marginal as time passes. Unless a good reason can be found to the contrary, it must now be time to question the monopoly of legitimacy that it seems to enjoy in public debate.

This is not just about recognising that different women want different types of lifestyles. Catherine Hakim has written much about how women will always be divided between those who like to be active in public affairs and paid work, and those who prefer to be active within their families, and how the test for social policy lies in reconciling these.[13] She makes a lot more sense than most commentators in this area. But the problem is surely bigger than this. Ultimately these differences between women revolve around what they think is important *for society*. The contemporary careerist thinks that modern society revolves around politics and the economy. It follows for her that being part of the workforce is what is important, and it is therefore unfair if men are allowed greater opportunities to perform the central roles. But for a woman with traditional values what is really important is family and community life, where existence is given its meaning and core moral values are formed and transmitted. For her the economy, along with other areas of public endeavour such as politics, science and the arts, organised religion and so on are there to serve and protect and enrich the lives of people like her family. So to her it does not matter if men have main control of them, so long as they remember what and *who* they are doing it all for!

These are the values which have been ignored.

The rise of the femocracy

It is intriguing to consider why this ancient and near-universal balance of power between men and women broke down in modern Britain. Hakim cites the development of industry, with the removal of (male-based) productive functions from inside households, where women could play a part in them, and their relocation in factories outside of family space and control.[14] This seems a reasonable account as far as it goes, but is surely not the only story. What seems to me likely to have been even more crucial is the development of the welfare state. This has an important political dimension too, and has reached within families and appropriated many of the powers formerly held by women themselves. A lot of the work taken on by middle class women since the second world war embraces very traditional women's concerns – of family life and human relations. Many women are now performing, in the welfare state, functions which their grandmothers would have carried out unpaid in the private. This is a source of some irritation to the *Women and Work Commission*, who say they would like to see girls becoming builders and car mechanics. But the Commissioners themselves are setting a very poor example to women here, and need to be careful what they say. The welfare state and employment of middle class women have expanded together. We all understand that.

A corollary of this which is not so often noted is that many of the activities and decisions previously carried out by mothers themselves, within the autonomy of their own homes, are now supervised by women paid by the state to do just that. The private realm has become a protectorate of the public. For young mothers, the position of the interfering mother-in-law, which could usually be kept within bounds by family checks and balances, has been superceded by that of the all-powerful social worker. It is processes like these, more than physical removal of male productive labour, which seem likely to make women feel that the centre of gravity is now 'out there' rather than in the home, and draw them into working themselves.

Equally, it is this process which seems to lead, perhaps inexorably, towards a system of social stratification among women. In the traditional model of society, where families are more independent, there is a sort of equality between women whatever the secular standing of their families. A woman's work as mother and centre of family life unites all women. But that soon gets lost when the state starts to organise families. Bureaucracy produces centralisation and class. Women's most prized asset has usually been control over their children; but the state can take that away too. The welfare state does not merely create jobs for women, it also structures these into a hierarchy of offices. All women with these jobs then exercise some authority, according to rank, over lower-status workers and, crucially, ordinary mothers. Mothers come at the bottom.[15] This is a prescription for conflict, as they have deep feelings about what is good for their children, and know what they will do for them if they can. That is what being a mother means.[16] They are hard-wired to resist interference.[17] So there seems almost bound to be tension between mothers and any public system which tries to orchestrate family life.

This tension will result in problems most often for lower class women. A middle class mother will probably have an important job herself, often enough within or linked to the state itself. If she does not herself, she will know somebody who does. So public officials and social workers will not push her around. She will not find her children being taken away for adoption. But for the lower classes, relations with femocrats have a hierarchical aspect. I suspect that this class problem is compounded further when women do not have male partners to support them and stick up for them, which is what mates are for. Thus at the very bottom of this hierarchy are poor single mothers, largely dependent on state charity and obliged to dance publicly to welfarist values which may often be at variance with how they would really like to live. There is a contradiction there, at the heart of single mothers' low morale, which presages that something in the system will soon have to give. The combination of opposed values with differential power is potentially quite explosive.

This particular conflict may even be inherent in the system itself, and largely unavoidable. It is arguable – though not in detail in the space available here – that femocrats at some level prefer to deal with single mothers than those with partners. A lot of the effort of the reformers who paved the way for the modern welfare state in Britain was devoted to discrediting men (as bullying control freaks) and articulating individual welfare entitlements for women/mothers that would not be dependent on husbands.[18]

To have direct access to mothers, and more immediate control over their children (whose wellbeing provides the speediest legitimisation for the exercise of power in the welfare state) must make life both simpler and more rewarding for the conscientious femocrat.[19] Displacing a mother's traditional best ally and supporter – her husband – pays off handsomely, and delivers a heavy blow to the private realm. This is sisterhood at work.

Restoring the private realm

Our national position at the moment is more than a little like that portrayed by Michael Young in his novel on the rise of the meritocracy. A soulless political class, devoted to education and performance, has asserted detailed, centralised control over people's lives. Family and community values have been squeezed out of British life. Or so the regime thinks. Unknown to them, a counter-revolutionary movement is brewing, formed around an alliance of young, middle class women who feel uncomfortable with how things are (the 'Girton Girls') and communitarian old men who can remember how it was before meritocracy was introduced. The story culminates and ends with hints of a bloodbath.

Much of that novel comes over now as a romantic fantasy, dreamt up in another world. For one thing, Girton Girls have been co-opted to our present regime and are far too busy running quangos and social services to brood over matters like the loss of community. In reality, we must wait for something more akin to the deputation of peasant women who are said to have persuaded Stalin to face up to the consequences of the New Family Policy. But what undoubtedly is parallel is the pervasive alienation of ordinary people from the operation of British democratic institutions and the looming sense of imminent collapse.

I do not share the view that this is because public servants and politicians are much less honest and devoted than they used to be. It is, I think, much more to do with the way that – as in Michael's novel – the public domain of politics and the economy over the last fifty years has eclipsed the *smaller* worlds of family and community, where people's lives are rooted. In traditional British society, as in most other times and places to a greater extent than here and now, the public realm existed to serve these smaller worlds. Now it seems to want to command them.[20]

So what can be done? Is it already too late?

It is never too late. Society is constantly undergoing renewal; and to start again we just need to stop doing what is not working.

The first step towards restoring the private realm is to give public recognition to marriage, and to reward it as the Conservatives are proposing. This is not social engineering by the state. It is in fact the opposite – that is getting the state to follow and endorse values and decisions arising in the private realm. It is about showing some respect to what ordinary people want; and it puts motherhood right back at the centre. Marriage is a relationship which gives people security in their lives, and – through ties of affinity – places them in a wider social framework. This helps to create order, which is good for all; not just women and children but men as well (or possibly even more so). When Disraeli quipped that 'Every woman should marry; and no man', he was alluding to the fact that men often feel ambivalent about marriage. But he understood, as his own novels show, that this is mainly because it can take quite a lot of personal experience for them to come to understand what most women will appreciate rather sooner.[21]

Although marriage is very much a product of the private realm, it does seem to need protection in the public domain. Certainly it is weakened – and with it private lives generally – if the state attaches penalties to it or (same thing really) gives advantages to people who are not married, as our present welfare regime does. The cost to the state of picking up lives that get broken through the absence of marriage means that it is very practical statecraft for a government to support it, and a sure sign of doctrinaire madness if it does not. But this is not the main reason why it should do it. The main reason is that this is essential to acknowledging the sovereignty of the people and their private values, which is long overdue.

Most of the other things that need doing are negative; that is, things which need *un*doing or avoiding. This comes down basically to stopping excessive state intervention in people's lives. The declared aim of such intervention is usually to make them happier. But this is a very uncertain outcome. What the micro-management of people's lives almost certainly does achieve is to make them more dependent, and the political class more powerful. It is better for a single mother for example to enable her to find a husband (by allowing the job market to respond to private realm impulses again, rather than social reform agendas) than it is to manage her through endless new benefit contracts and initiatives.

Lately the government has started to take family ties into consideration in its policies, by rewarding some very specific family activities. For example there is the pension credit scheme for people who are involved in caring for relatives. I accept that this may all be motivated by a respect for family life; but I have my doubts about going much further down this road. It just does not seem to be a good principle to pay people for doing particular things in the private realm in this way. This is not just because it may stop people doing things that they are *not* paid for, or may annoy or discourage those who do not qualify for payment. These are real dangers. But I think that the main reason I have doubts is that by paying for these things to be done the state is effectively asserting its superiority, and right to determine which bits of the private realm are useful to it.

It is only during a time such as we are in now, when the public domain is rampant, that people can even imagine that this sort of close intervention could be a good idea. For this really is social engineering. If payments are being made in order to get people to do things that they are not really inclined to do, then it is probably better if they are not done anyway. If, as I suspect, they are being made in order to support people who do want to carry them out but have difficulty doing so because they lack resources – that is, because of poverty – then some more general way of alleviating poverty should be found: as in higher state pensions (which would be easily possible in this country if less were spent on social engineering) or a higher minimum wage. Far better an enabling state than interventionist.

143

The whole point about the private realm is that it is where people can decide among themselves how to use their resources and spend their time. And they will look after each other if they are allowed to and able. In a country like Italy, families and the private realm are strong. The government does not intervene in how things are done, though some politicians there would like it to. It confines itself to looking after people who don't have families, and supports the private realm in a very general way by paying a reasonable state pension to ensure that all families have resources coming in. This is all it needs to do. Older generations in families pass on much of their income to younger family members. Even though it is older people who receive the money, everyone benefits. What the state does, in effect, is to water the roots of extended family life. It does not attempt to micro-manage behaviour. And the result is a much more healthy community life, with happier people than you will find in Britain. The politicians are not obviously more honest and devoted. But people are not alienated from the system. This is because the public domain knows its place.

We could be more like that again here in Britain. I think it is what a lot of women want.

Notes to Chapters

Notes to Chapter One:

[1] Economist, 2010.

[2] There is democracy in this. As I have argued myself, "[A national sample survey] complements other consultations. Mass elections give all citizens a voice, but only on generalised platforms. Constituency surgeries listen in depth, but few get an ear. Sample surveys, though, can speak in detail for a whole nation. To the right to vote is added a calculable chance of becoming part of a computed general will." Dench, 2001.

[3] Rathbone, 1924.

[4] Miriam David, 1996.

[5] In retrospect this can be seen as of special value to men, by giving them motivations within the powerful private realm which underpinned their activity in the public realm. See Dench 1996.

[6] Gorer, 1955.

[7] Gorer, 1970.

[8] The *Women in Employment Survey*, (WES) commissioned by the Dept. of Employment and reported by Martin & Roberts, 1984.

[9] Witherspoon, 1985.

[10] Dench, 2009.

[11] That is, produces a 98% to 99% overlap of cases.

[12] And also showed quite a difference even between 1984 and 1987.

[13] Hinds & Jarvis 2000.

[14] E.g. Coote *et al* 1990, and Hewitt 1993.

[15] See Scott, 1990 for details.

[16] See Thomson, 1995.

[17] The base numbers become rather small when we concentrate on these sub-groups, and caution is needed. But the pattern of responses here is so consistent with other findings that it should not simply be discounted.

[18] See Layard & Dunn, 2009, and Joseph Rowntree Foundation, 2009. Concern had been prompted by a Unesco report (q.v.) in 2007 which showed the level of well-being of British children as being below that of most other rich countries.

[19] Unlike for most other variables, there is no suggestion of rebound *before* 2006. But figures here do suggest some flattening after 1998.

145

So, even though we only have a single year's evidence, it does look quite likely that recovery is indeed now underway.

[20] "Four out of five women working full-time said [in a YouGov survey, during 2009] that they would choose not to work, if they didn't have to for financial reasons." Odone, 2009, p. 13

[21] Hakim, 1996. p.206

[22] The Economist article treats 'motherhood' simply as a problem faced by less fortunate working women.

[23] Note that the happiest of all seem to be housewives who have *very* part-time jobs, under 10 hours a week, and who are therefore classified for most purposes by BSA as *not* working. But the numbers of these are too small to permit reliable separate analysis.

[24] Ashford, 1987

[25] Witherspoon, 1988

[26] Witherspoon & Prior, 1991, p. 132

[27] Thomson, 1995, p. 83

[28] Crompton & Lyonette, 2008

[29] Crompton et al, 2003, p.162

[30] Crompton & Lyonette, 2008, p.54

[31] Maushart, 1999.

[32] Hrdy, 1999.

NOTES TO CHAPTER TWO:

[1] See Dench, 1996

[2] Hakim, 1996. pp206-7

[3] 'Lone' and 'single' are used interchangeably in this analysis.

[4] Dench, 2009

[5] Brown *et al*, 2004

[6] In 2006, when there was a group of questions dealing with LAT, 34% of lone mothers indicated that they did have such partners. But we cannot tell how full a tally this actually represents, as many people in these relationships make a point of not mentioning it to social researchers.

[7] Gingerbread, 2007, page 5

[8] Please note that the figures used in tables 2.7 and 2.8 are based on the author's interpretation of BSA data, and are not taken *directly* from BSA questions. BSA response categories and interviewer

instructions relating to marital and domestic status have been changed a number of times; but at no point have they produced unambiguous, direct estimates of the proportion of people who have never lived with a partner. Any such figures inevitably involve interpretation of other data. The interpretation used for figures here is based on the assumption that most people, especially mothers, who have lived as married with a partner and then split up will regard their subsequent status as *separated* rather than *single.'*

[9] Walby, 1990

[10] See the discussion in de Waal, 2008

[11] Dench, 1996

[12] See the figures given in Rowthorn & Webster, 2008

[13] Rathbone, 1924

[14] An almost universal situation. See Wilson, 1987

[15] Rowthorn & Webster, 2008 and Hakim, 1996.

[16] Note that even men with partners aged 50-64 are now less active in the labour market than women aged 50-59.

[17] Also some young women may be using single motherhood as a way of taking a stand against dominant, pro-work values.

NOTES TO CHAPTER THREE

[1] See McFarlane, 1978

[2] Laslett, 1977

[3] Anderson, 1972; and Hibbert, 1987

[4] There was no role for grandfathers in this system.

[5] Uhlendorf & Kirby, 1998

[6] Kosberg, 1992; and Lewis and Meredith, 1988

[7] As noted by a number of contributors to Dench, 2000

[8] Attias-Donfut & Segalen, 1998

[9] Written up in detail in Dench & Ogg, 2002.

[10] A type of situation discussed by Troll, 1985

[11] *Op cit.* 2002, p 151

[12] Bengtson & Achenbaum, 1993

[13] See the discussion on this in Dench & Ogg, chapter 4.

[14] See Dench & Ogg, 2002, for more detail.

[15] Co-residence these days is mainly a matter of children continuing to live in the parental home, rather than elderly parents moving in

with their children.

[16] McGlone, Park & Roberts, 1996, p.59

[17] See also the more general argument in Dench 2009

[18] Thomson, 1995

[19] Grandparents Plus, 2009a

[20] This conclusion, for simplicity, does rather treat grandparental childcare as an undivided entity. In practice of course single mothers are often confined to help from *maternal* grandparents, while mothers with partners can usually expect help from both sets. So the moderate amount of 'extra' grandparental help which mothers get when they are single may represent a great deal more when considered from the active grandparents' point of view. See Dench & Ogg, 2002, chapter 6.

[21] DCSF, 2007

[22] Willetts, 2010

[23] Martin & Roberts, 1984

[24] Dench & Ogg, 2002, chapter 9

[25] Ibid

[26] Ibid, pp 91-94

[27] Ibid

[28] Ibid p95

[29] Park & Roberts, 2002, p204

[30] E.g. Future Foundation, 2000

[31] Op cit p98

[32] People in all societies give priority to the needs of children, and older generations are usually willing to sacrifice themselves for the sake of younger. Accordingly, parents tend to put themselves out much more for their children than they do for their parents.

[33] Arber & Attias-Donfut, 2000

[34] Brown *et al*, 2004

[35] From tables 6.5a and 6.6

[36] The figures for 1998 and 2006-08 are however based on slightly different questions. In 1998 respondents were asked about one randomly selected grandchild. So where they had more than one child with children we do not know much about the others. In the 2006-08 data they are responding to a question about whether *any* of their grandchildren's parents are not together. So there is a slightly higher chance of a positive response.

[37] But see previous footnote, anyway

[38] Phillips, 1999

[39] Note that women recorded very high rates of working in 1998 – levels not reached again for some years. This was possibly a response to the election of New Labour. But this spike makes assessment of longer term change in relation to that year very difficult.

[40] However, the work rate of lone MGMs holds up better in the most recent period than that of lone PGMs; possibly because some of them are helping out their daughters financially.

[41] The actual question in 1998 refers to the 'mother of your grandchildren'. For MGMs this will have been their daughters.

[42] The bases are quite small here; but not so small that differences of this magnitude could be due to chance.

Notes to Chapter Four

[1] See Hinds & Jarvis, 2000

[2] Dench, 2009

[3] Willetts, 2010

[4] The working definitions of class used here to compile these tables are not given by BSA. BSA itself does not have a 'class' variable. For the purposes of tables which follow here, Middle Class embraces people with professional and higher managerial occupations; the Intermediate Class contains lower managerial, administrative and technical workers, and Working Class covers manual and routine jobs.

[5] Dench, 2009

[6] This is not specified in this table, which includes childless women as well as mothers – and as a result makes housewives look less content than most are. There is a dilemma here. We *need* to include childless women in this table, in order to have enough cases to draw reliable conclusions from it. If we do instead focus just on mothers with dependent children the four column base numbers drop to 81, 104, 36 and 83. That is, they go down very heavily *except* for part-time workers and housewives, which is what most mothers tend to be. And, very significantly, it is these two categories which, for mothers, emerge as considerably happier than the others – with the top row 'very happy' now ready as 54, 72, 46 and 61. Given that the

pattern of figures for *mothers* is otherwise very similar to that for *all women of working age,* we can perhaps take this second set of figures a bit more seriously than if it were standing completely alone. It does have some credibility. But the proviso is important; we should not let it stand alone.

[7] Some of the figures in this table are possibly not very dependable, basically because so *few* middle and intermediate class women are not working that the bases to these two columns are very small.

[8] Crompton & Lyonette, 2008

[9] And this vital community work arguably includes having a male partner and thereby helping to create a motivational system enabling men to lead orderly, productive lives. The rise of single motherhood, which spurns this task, should be seen as part of the wider breakdown of community life in Britain. See my book on how men are transformed by family life; Dench, 1996.

[10] Nor does it include 'don't know' responses or failures to answer.

[11] (including 'no party')

[12] Shils & Young, 1953

[13] Hakim, 1996

[14] *ibid*

[15] See the discussion in Odone, 2009

[16] Hrdy, 1999

[17] Just look at the mother's expression on the book front cover!

[18] This included making family allowances payable from the outset to *mothers.*

[19] It would also help to explain why social workers have been so eager to air-lift teenage single mothers out of their own mothers' households, and teenage girls generally from their mothers' influence.

[20] As anticipated by Michael's lesser-known work, Young, 1948

[21] In passing we should note very carefully that middle class Britain, for all its scornful noise about not needing to support marriage any more, is in practice much more likely to *get* married than working class Britain. This is of course closely related to the fact that middle class men have jobs and incomes that make them reliable breadwinners. The opinion-forming classes do not understand about the problems of men in humbler circumstances, as this is outside of their own experience.

REFERENCES

Anderson, M. (1972), *Family Structure in Nineteenth Century Lancashire*, Cambridge: Cambridge University Press

Arber, S. & C. Attias-Donfut (eds) (2000), *The Myth of Generational Conflict*, London: Routledge

Ashford, S. (1987), 'Family matters', in R. Jowell *et al* (eds) *British Social Attitudes: The 1987 report*, Aldershot: Gower

Attias-Donfut, C. & M. Segalen (1998), *Grands-Parents: La famille à travers les générations*, Paris: Odile Jacob

Barker, P., E. Bauer, B. Brown, G. Dench, N. Green & P. Hall (2002), 'The meaning of the Jubilee', *ICS Working Paper* No. 1

Bengtson, V. L. & W. A. Achenbaum (eds) (1993), *The Changing Contract Across the Generations*, New York: de Gruyter

Brown, B. & G. Dench (2004), *Valuing Informal Care: What mothers of young children want*, London: Hera Trust

Candy, L. (2009), 'A very unlikely feminist', *Daily Mail*, June 22

Coote, A., H. Harman & P. Hewitt (1990) *The Family Way: A new approach to policy-making*, London: IPPR

Crompton, R., M. Brockman & R. D. Wiggins (2003), A woman's place... Employment and family life for men and women', in A. Park *et al* (eds) *British Social Attitudes: the 20th report*, London: Sage

Crompton, R. & C. Lyonette (2007), 'Are we all working too hard? Women, men, and changing attitudes to employment', in A. Park *et al* (eds) *British Social Attitudes: The 23th report*, London: Sage

Crompton, R. & C. Lyonette (2008), 'Who does the housework? The division of labour within the home', in A. Park *et al* (eds) *British Social Attitudes: The 24th report*, London: Sage

David, M. E. (1997), 'Family roles from the dawn to the dusk of the New Elizabethan Era', in G. Dench (ed) *Rewriting the Sexual Contract*, London: ICS

DCSF. (2007) *The Children's Plan; Building brighter futures*, London: HMSO

De Waal, A. (2008), *Second Thoughts on the Family*, London: Civitas

Dench, G. (1996), *Transforming Men*, New Brunswick: Transaction

Dench, G. (ed) (2000). *Grandmothers of the Revolution*, London: Hera Trust

Dench, G. (2001), 'Reflection of the national soul', *Times Higher*, August 3

Dench, G. (2009), 'Exploring parents' views', in A. Park *et al* (eds), *British Social Attitudes, the 25th report*, London: Sage

Dench, G., J. Ogg & K Thomson (1999), 'The role of grandparents', in R. Jowell *et al* (eds), *British Social Attitudes, the 16th report*, Aldershot: Ashgate

Dench, G. & J. Ogg (2002), *Grandparenting in Britain*, London: ICS

Economist, (2010) 'Women and work: We did it!', *The Economist*, January 2nd – 8th

Future Foundation (2000), *Complicated Lives*, London: Future Foundation

Gingerbread (2007), *One Parent Families Today: The Facts*, London: National Council for One Parent Families

Gorer, G. (1955), *Exploring English Character*, London: Cresset

Gorer, G. (1970), *Sex and Marriage in England Today*, London: Cresset

Grandparents Plus (2009a), *Rethinking Family Life*, London: Grandparents Plus

Grandparents Plus (2009b), *The Poor Relation? Grandparental care: where older people's poverty and child poverty meets*, London: Grandparents Plus

Hakim, C. (1996), *Key Issues in Women's Work: Female heterogeneity and the polarisation of women's employment*, London: Athlone

Hewitt, P. (1993) *About Time*, London: IPPR

Hibbert, C. (1987), *The English: A social history 1066-1945*, London: Harper Collins

Hinds, K. & L. Jarvis (2000),'The gender gap', in R. Jowell et al (eds), *British Social Attitudes: The 17th report*, London: Sage

Hrdy, S. (1999), *Mother Nature*, London: Chatto & Windus

Joseph Rowntree Foundation (2009), *Contemporary Social Evils*, Bristol: Policy

Kosberg, J (ed) (1992), *Family Care of the Elderly*, Newbury Park, CA: Sage

Laslett, P. (1977), *Family Life in Earlier Generations*, Cambridge: Cambridge University Press

Layard, R. & J. Dunn (2009), *A Good Childhood*, London: Penguin

References

Lewis, J & B. Meredith (1988), *Daughters Who Care*, London: Routledge

Maushart, S. (1999), *The Mask of Motherhood: How becoming a mother changes everything and why we pretend it doesn't*, New York: The New Press

Martin, J. & C. Roberts (1984), *Women and Employment: A lifetime perspective*, London: HMSO

McFarlane, A. (1978), *The Origins of Individualism in England*, Cambridge: Cambridge University Press

McGlone, F., A. Park & C. Roberts (1996), 'Relative values: kinship and friendship', in R. Jowell *et al* (eds), *British Social Attitudes, the 13th report*, Aldershot: Dartmouth

Morgan, P. (1995), *Farewell to the Family?* London: IEA

Murray, C. (1984), *Losing Ground*, New York: Basic Books

Nock, S. L. (1998), *Marriage in Men's Lives*, New York: Oxford University Press

Odone, C. (2009), *What Women Want*, London: CPS

Park, A. & C. Roberts (2002), 'The ties that bind', in A. Park *et al* (eds), *British Social Attitudes: the 19th report*, London: Sage

Phillips, M. (1999), *The Sex-Change Society*, London: Social Market Foundation

Rathbone, E. (1924), *The Disinherited Family*, London: Edward Arnold

Rowthorn, R & D. Webster (2008), 'Male worklessness and the rise of lone parenthood in Great Britain', *Cambridge Journal of Regions, Economy and Society* n. 1

Scott, J. (1990), 'Women and the family', in R. Jowell *et al* (eds), *British Social Attitudes: the 7th report*, Aldershot: Gower

Scott, J., M. Braun & D. Alwin (1993) 'The family way', in R. Jowell *et al* (eds) *International Social Attitudes: the 10th BSA report*, Aldershot: Dartmouth

Scott, J., M. Braun & D. Alwin (1998) 'Partner, parent, worker: family and gender roles', in R. Jowell *et al* (eds) *British – and European - Social Attitudes: the 15th report*, Aldershot: Ashgate

Shils, E. & M. Young (1955), 'The meaning of the Coronation', *Sociological Review*, NS. 3

Thomson, K. (1995), 'Working mothers: choice or circumstance?' in R. Jowell *et al* (eds), *British Social Attitudes: the 12th report*, Aldershot: Dartmouth

Toynbee, A. & D.Ikeda (1989), *Choose Life*, Oxford: Oxford University Press

Troll, L. (1985), 'The contingencies of grandparenting', in V.L. Bengtson & J. F. Robertson (eds) *Grandparenthood*, Beverley Hills: Sage

Uhlenberg, P. & J. B. Kirby (1998), 'Grandparenthood over time: historical and demographic trends', in M. Szinovacz (ed) *Handbook on Grandparenthood*, Westport: Greenwood

UNESCO (2007), *Measuring and Monitoring the Well-being of Young Children Around the World*

Walby, S. (1990), *Theorising Patriarchy*, Oxford: Blackwell

Willetts, D. (2010), *The Pinch: How the baby boomers took their children's future,*

Wilson, W. J. (1987), *The Truly Disadvantaged*, Chicago: Chicago University Press

Witherspoon, S. (1985), 'Sex roles and gender issues', in R. Jowell *et al* (eds), *British Social Attitudes: the 1985 report*, Aldershot: Gower

Witherspoon, S. (1988), 'Interim report: A woman's work', in R. Jowell *et al* (eds), *British Social Attitudes: the 5th report*, Aldershot: Gower

Witherspoon, S. & G. Prior (1991), 'Working mothers: Free to choose?', in R. Jowell *et al* (eds), *British Social Attitudes: the 8th report*, Aldershot: Dartmouth

Young, M. (1948), Small man, big world, *Towards Tomorrow*, No. 4

Geoff Dench is a sociologist who has written mainly in the areas of family relations and local community studies. He is a senior fellow of the Young Foundation, and a visiting professor at Greenwich University.